SELF-HELP AMONG THE ELDERLY

FORMAL AND INFORMAL SUPPORT SYSTEMS

BESSIE WRIGHT

GARLAND PUBLISHING, INC.
NEW YORK & LONDON / 1994

Library of Congress Cataloging-in-Publication Data

Wright, Bessie, 1939–
    Self-help among the elderly : formal and informal support systems /
Bessie Wright.
        p.   cm. — (Garland studies on the elderly in America)
    Includes bibliographical references (p.   ) and index.
    ISBN 0–8153–1613–5 (alk. paper)
    1. Aged—Care—United States.   2. Aged—United States—Social
networks.   3. Self-help groups—United States.   I. Title. II. Series.
HV1461.W75   1994
362.6—dc20   93–48665
                                                                      CIP

Printed on acid-free, 250-year-life paper
Manufactured in the United States of America

To the memory of my parents

Porter and Bessie H. Wright

CONTENTS

TABLES

PREFACE

Most preface statements are readily skipped over, much like today's wisdom is turned down in favor of "the quick fix" and "the sound byte." I often say to young people, "from whom do you get your wisdom?" Most give a quizzical look to which I suspect that they are not sure what wisdom is, and for clarification for this publication, let me suggest here that wisdom is, "good practical judgment, common sense and a high degree of knowledge."

What better way to provide self-help among the elderly than that of bringing peer wisdom of the elderly into play. Through interaction with those who have experienced what the affected must go through, the elderly affected will have available to them the ability to reflect, compare, understand, and impose reality testing on short term or long term illness. Indeed, what better exchange of ideas than those that can be found in peer discussions of how he or she overcomes a similar social/medical problem currently plaguing someone who is looking for support and/or answers to some medical enigma.

As our society seems more and more eager to give over to institutions, those social practices that in earlier times were provided by significant others, we seem to have lost some humility in the process. We have farmed out mildly dysfunctional children, adults, and especially the elderly to public and private institutions for care on the one hand and reaped social isolation for these individuals on the other. It seems to me that Professor Bessie Wright's material on self-help should move policy makers to consider self-help as the chief modality in fulfilling the social and medical needs of the elderly as we approach the 21st century--a group whose population has increased by 232 percent since 1960 and continues to grow at an even faster rate. But even more important, we must begin to use the wisdom of the elderly to bring back a measure of civility to society at large. An example of this aspect of the elderly as caregivers centers on a research project that I launched some years ago whereby the elderly were recruited to provide values clarification and educational skills to kindergarten children and provide role modeling for their parents in the formal setting of the public school. And while the children and parents relished the results of the wisdom of the elderly which provided them with instruction and insights, what was, perhaps, more powerful, was the sense of contributing; of giving back to society, embraced by the elderly in the program.

From whom do we get our wisdom? The elderly of course.

James A. Malone, PhD
Professor of Counseling
John Jay College of Criminal Justice
CUNY

ACKNOWLEDGMENTS

I thank Drs. Abraham Monk, James Jones (deceased) and Barbara Morrison for their support and assistance during the preparation and completion of the initial research project.

I am grateful to the administration, staff, and members of the Associated Young Men and Women Hebrew Association, New York, for providing support and sharing their resources during the planning and implementation of this research project.

A special appreciation is extended to Carolyn Tonge, Dr. Flora Miller, and Esther Owens for patiently reading this manuscript and making valid comments. Special thanks to Dr. James Malone for writing the preface.

Sincere thanks to my family and friends who always encouraged me to achieve. Finally, a special appreciation is extended to friends and colleagues at John Jay College of Criminal Justice--Vice President Roger Witherspoon, Dean Norma Brady, and especially to Dr. Rubie Malone, my friend, for all of their support and encouragement throughout my efforts to finalize this book.

I
INTRODUCTION

A major concern of government as well as private-sector researchers and planners in the United States today is fulfilling the economic, physical, and social needs of the elderly. By 1990, the elderly population (that is, those 65 years of age or older) was over 31.1 million, representing 12.5 percent[1] of all Americans. This group will continue to grow at a rapid pace--accompanied by a corresponding growth in its members' dependence on government and private groups to help fulfill their needs. As early as the 1960s the facts concerning the dramatic increase, both in the numbers of old people and their higher longevity, became public knowledge. In fact, writers began to focus on families where both children and parents were in the aging phase of the life cycle.[2] Today, four generation families are becoming a common phenomena. This means that more people in their fifties and sixties will have surviving parents, aunts and uncles.[3]

Demographic information on the elderly population points out that during the twentieth century the total population has tripled. During this same time, the 65 and over population has increased tenfold, from 3.1 million at the turn of the century to 31.1 million in 1990. Projections are that by the middle of the twenty-first century this population will more than double to 69 million and that the 85 and above population will be the fastest growing. According to Taeuber, this group has increased by 232 percent since 1960, compared to an increase of 89 percent for those in the 65 and over population.[4] While this reflects only a little above 1 percent of the American population, that number is large enough to provide a major impact on this country's health and social service systems. The discussion above indicates that the aging population continues to experience the greatest increase among its oldest members. Thus, a reasonable expectation would be that this population's physical, mental, and social needs will impact significantly upon the providers of such services.

Studies have confirmed that the family remains the greatest and most cost effective source of care for the elderly. The New York State Office for the Aging's report on Family Caregiving and the Elderly, based on a thorough review of family care-giving, states that "older people in this country receive the majority of their care from family members."[5] Research has established that the family provides 80 to 90 percent of long-term personal care, household assistance, and help in transportation and shopping.[6] It should be noted, however, that care for the elderly is often provided with very substantial economic and social costs sustained by the family involved, especially for families where the elderly person is not residing in the household. Often, the family members providing the care have to travel great distances to visit the elderly person. In addition, these providers generally have children and spouses themselves who impose demands, and/or both of the spouses in the caregiver's household may be employed, thus placing a further strain on the time and energy of family members who provide care for the elderly. Studies have documented that women provide a significant amount of the personal care to the elderly family members. Some are required to leave work earlier than originally planned in order to care for parents which can affect retirement benefits for their own old age.[7] Furthermore, substantial numbers of the elderly do not have a spouse and/or children; thus, a critical need exists to identify additional and alternative modes of care for the ever-growing elderly population.

Gerontologists and other researchers have indicated that even with the growing proportion of elderly in this country, 95 percent still live, at any given time, in the community. These persons have need for both the formal support systems (government agencies and other social services agencies) and informal support systems such as families, neighbors, friends and additional significant others in the focal person's life who are not professional helpers. Researchers, like Litwak, and Cantor and Mayer, argue that it is both necessary and possible for families to have concurrently access to formal organizations and informal support systems.[8] The formal organizations provide the economic and expert assistance necessary during the provision of services while the informal support systems "provide diffused relations and long-term commitments."[9] The informal support systems in this study, also referred to as 'self-help groups or activities' focus on those activities in which individuals and/or groups of individuals engage to provide mutual support aid to themselves and others during the course of daily life activities.

The literature has included recommendations by many, for example, Monk and Califano,[10] that new ways need to be developed to help meet the social service needs of the elderly such as needs for transportation, home management, shopping, entertainment and companionship. All of these areas, and many others are vital to the physical, economic and mental health of the elderly person. With the increased mobility of society in the late twentieth century, there has been a significant increase in the number of self-help or informal mutual support groups. This proliferation of self-help activities throughout the country has received widespread attention. Much of it is reported and discussed by Gartner and Riessman[11] in "The Self-Help Revolution." Programs exist at all age levels and with various orientations to meet people's needs and to help them in adjusting to critical physical, psychological, or economic circumstances. Self-help groups, for example, are formed to help those who are terminally ill prepare for death, as well as to help others provide the support necessary for basic daily living.

Self-help groups have made major contributions toward dealing with problems which cannot usually be dealt with effectively by other social institutions, while at the same time they provide people with the opportunity for helping roles. The data suggest that increasingly older people are helping each other informally or in an organized manner with or without the help of social service professionals.[12] In fact, Cantor pointed out as a result of her inner-city study in New York City during the early 1970s that:

> The United States government provides the floor of basic services for older people in such crucial areas as income maintenance, housing, health and transportation. But the family and significant others retain in a city like New York, considerable importance in meeting the more idiosyncratic human social support needs of the individual.[13]

It has been established that the elderly are our fastest growing segment of the population. This growth has been accompanied by a corresponding rise in the cost of providing services and economic support to them. Therefore, innovative, cost-effective programs in service delivery must be developed. Katz discussed the need for programs to prevent loneliness, to deal with death and dying, to get and keep the aged involved in the activities of their communities and to maintain good physical, mental and dental health by preventing illness as much as possible.[14] Writers such as Baker, Dory, and Litwak have suggested self-help organizations as alternative caregiving systems, that these systems are applicable in programs for the elderly and that these groups can work together or side by side to provide comprehensive services to the elderly.[15]

Dory saw self-help activities as an opportunity for older Americans to coalesce and get things done, as a system of support in crisis situations as well as a way of creating a new attitude toward aging. She urged the elderly to resist the notion that there is a time when they should cease to be active, have no important work to do, and when their days are consumed only with leisure activity. Instead, she encouraged them to work toward integrating their lifestyle at every age level so that they could experience a healthy balance between work and leisure.[16] Self-help groups can be instrumental in this process as they have been in similar situations of life-style reorganization.

Self-help activities have increasingly been used by the elderly. The aged are acting on their own behalf to identify factors mitigating against them and exploring additional services which allow them to lead fuller and more active lives.

PURPOSE OF THE STUDY

The intent of this study is to provide information which will assist in understanding the effective use of self-help roles and/or informal support systems among the elderly and at the same time provide evidence of the continuing need for social service agencies to work with the elderly. Specifically, this study profiles the elderly participants in self-help groups at two social activities' centers in New York City. The study's aims are to describe (1) help the elderly receive from family and friends; (2) help the elderly give to children; (3) the relationship of demographic characteristics of the elderly to patterns of self-help activity; (4) the correlation between actual use of different self-help activities; and (5) the correlation between the elderly's perception of helping sources (i.e., self, friends, relatives or social agency) and actual use of self-help activities. Chapter II reviews the literature and theoretical considerations relating to the subject while Chapter III covers the research design and methodology including operational definitions of study variables, sampling, data collection and instrumentation, limitations of the research sample, and data analysis procedures; Chapter IV presents the research findings, and Chapter V, the concluding chapter, reviews the findings, their implications, and discusses recommendations for future research.

Notes

1. Cynthia M. Taeuber, *Sixty-Five Plus in America*, Current Population Reports, Special Studies (Washington, DC: U.S. Department of Commerce, Economics and Statistics Administration. Bureau of the Census, 1992), 23-178.

2. E.M. Brody, "The Aging Family," *The Gerontologist*, 6, no. 4 (December 1969): 201-206.

3. Taeuber, *Sixty-Five Plus in America*, 2-12.

4. Ibid., 2-4, 5.

5. New York State Office for the Aging, *Family Caregiving and the Elderly: Policy Recommendations and Research Findings* (Monograph), March 1983, 1.

6. A.M. Jette, S.L. Tennstedt, and L.G. Branch, "Stability of Informal Long-Term Care, *Journal of Aging and Health*, 4, no. 2 (May 1992): 193 - 211; and R.J. Taylor, "Receipt of Support from Family among Black Americans: Demographic and Familial Difference," *Journal of Marriage and the Family*, 48 (February 1986): 67-77.

7. Taeuber, *Sixty-Five Plus in America*; and M. Jocelyn Armstrong and Karen S. Goldsteen, "Friendship Support Patterns of Older American Women," *Journal of Aging Studies*, 4, no. 4 (1990): 391-404.

8. Eugene Litwak, *Helping the Elderly: The Complementary Roles of Informal Networks and Formal Systems* (New York: Guilford Press), 262-263; and Marjorie H. Cantor and Mary J. Mayer, "Factors in Differential Utilization of Services by Urban Elderly" (paper presented at the 28th Annual Scientific Meeting of the Gerontological Society, Louisville, Kentucky, October 29, 1975), 3.

9. Litwak, *Helping the Elderly*, 3.

10. Abraham Monk, "Family Supports in Old Age," *Social Work*, 24, no. 6 (November 1979): 533-538; and Joseph A. Califano, "The Aging of America: Questions for a Four Generation Society," *The Annals of the American Academy of Political and Social Science*, July 1978, 96-108.

11. Alan Gartner and Frank Reissman, eds., *The Self-Help Revolution* (New York: Human Science Press, 1984).

12. Beth B. Hess, "Self-Help Among the Aged," *Social Policy*, 7, no. 3 (November/December 1976): 55-62.

13. Marjorie H. Cantor, "The Formal and Informal Social Support System of Older New Yorkers" (paper presented at Symposium: The City: A Viable Environment for the Elderly? 10th International Congress of Gerontology, Jerusalem, Israel, June 1975), 4.

14. Solomon Katz, "Anthropological Perspective on Aging," *The Annals of the American Academy of Political and Social Science*, July 1978, 1-12.

15. Frank Baker, "The Interface Between Professional and Natural Support Systems," *Clinical Social Work Journal*, 5, no. 2 (1977): 139-148; Frances J. Dory, *Building Self-help Groups Among Older Persons* (New York: New Careers Training Laboratory, Center for Advanced Study in Education, Graduate School and University Center, City University of New York, 1979), Part II, 13-20; and Eugene Litwak, *Helping the Elderly*, 262.

16. Dory, *Building Self-help Groups Among Older Persons*, 20.

II
SELF-HELP AND THE EXCHANGE THEORY

In reviewing the literature of self-help activities, several important themes emerged. This chapter consists of the following: (1) a theoretical definition of self-help groups; (2) information on the orientations and levels of development of self-help groups which assist people in adjusting to various physical, psychological, and economic conditions; (3) background information on the historical development of various self-help groups and organizations in this country; and (4) the role of self-help groups versus formal service delivery organizations including the net gains and drawbacks of both.

Emphasis also is placed on exchange theory which was the theoretical framework for this study.

THEORETICAL DEFINITION OF
SELF-HELP GROUPS

The *Encyclopedia of Social Work* defines self-help as, "the provision of aid to oneself. By extension, collectives of individuals formed into self-help groups provide mutual aid to each other around common problems."[1] For the purpose of the present study, self-help was defined as "those activities in which individuals and/or groups of individuals engage when providing mutual aid to themselves and others during the course of daily life activities and interactions."[2]

An important characteristic of formal social service organizations is that consumers, or clients, should be the focus of the services, and they should become involved in serving themselves. Therefore, the characteristics of a typical self-help group would complement those of a social service organization.

A number of writers have recently begun to systematically review and organize the literature on the various self-help groups and activities, attempting to develop some rationale for the development of these groups in modern society.[3] Throughout history, people have used their connections with small groups--with family, kinfolk, and peers--for stability in stormy and difficult times, thus helping to ensure their own survival.

The review and organization of the literature on self-help have centered on the groups (e.g., Gamblers Anonymous, Mended Heart, Inc., etc.) which have some type of formal structure as the focus of study rather than on the individual. These groups have generally attempted to bring the individual back to some former state of "well-being" or "equilibrium." There has not been much focus on the exchanges between individuals whether on a one-to-one level or in a group context, which prevents the deterioration of their current status. More recently the focus of self-help groups has expanded to embrace any group of persons sharing a similar concern or outlook. They embrace a key social work principle of helping the client to determine personal goals and implement a plan of action toward goal attainment. Self-help group members engage in activities of exchange with each others around common goals and in response to commonly perceived needs.[4] These exchanges which are also identified as "mutual help" forms of assistance are the intent of this study. Even though the study was implemented in two group settings, the focus was on the more spontaneous activities of the individuals in these settings.

As Katz and Bender have pointed out, people need to recognize themselves as well as to be recognized by the larger society: it is vitally important that people both discover themselves and be accepted for what they are. People need to be valued, to experience and to share with each other.[5] Self-help movements have, therefore, evolved in order to fulfill some of these self-identity needs. In the past, many of these services have been and continue to be performed by the family, the church, the neighborhood, and the community.

Self-help groups are viewed as part of the phenomena of the "service society" where macroeconomic forces impose new forms of services with a necessarily different division of labor to accommodate the demands of a post-industrial era. These self-help groups are viewed as an expression of the democratic ideal and as a model of consumer participation.

Gartner and Riessman, in their review of the literature on self-help activities, focused on human-services-oriented mutual aid centered on the small group. They defined these self-help groups as small voluntary structures where people provide mutual aid for the achievement of a specific purpose. Commonly, peers form a self-help group to satisfy a shared need, solve a shared problem and bring about the desired change. In addition, the group founders generally perceive that their shared needs are not and cannot be met by the formal service-giving agencies.[6]

Self-help groups also are perceived by many observers as an intrinsic part of the expanding peer-oriented helping networks and associations such as peer counseling, children teaching children, and self-help by the elderly. Killilea has stated that much of the self-help activity, along with much of the other human potential and growth movements, can be seen as a part of a search for "an appreciative system sufficiently widely shared to mediate communication, sufficiently apt to guide action and sufficiently acceptable to make personal experience bearable."[7] Killilea also has discussed overall interpretations of self-help groups as well as the relationship of these groups to the formal care-giving system.

An aspect of living which seems critical to the elderly at this time in their lives is that their physical and economic independence declines as they age. Obviously, there is a need for different support systems for the elderly. In her work, Killilea discusses (among other topics): (1) support systems; (2) alternative caregiving systems; (3) expressive/social influence groups; and (4) a vehicle to aid in coping with life-cycle transitions.[8] Let us examine these four categories.

Support systems. Caplan defined support system as composing an enduring pattern of continuous or intermittent ties that play a significant part in maintaining the psychological and physical integrity of the individual over time.

Support systems, then, are bonds between individuals or groups that improve adaptive ability in coping with short-term crisis and life transitions as well as long-term challenges, stresses, and privations. Caplan suggested several ways in which adaptiveness can be enhanced:

(1) by promoting the mastery of one's emotions; (2) by defining problems and the options for dealing with them; and (3) by fostering a realistic self-image that encourages self-evaluation and heightens self-esteem.[9]

Alternative caregiving systems. These may be defined as self-help groups organized independently of the formal caregiving system (e.g., Alcoholics Anonymous, Mended Hearts, Gamblers Anonymous, Vietnam Veterans Against the War). A study by Traunstein and Steinman of self-help organizations in an upper New York State community suggested that many people are serviced by their peers in a fashion which parallels, compliments and, in many instances, competes with the social welfare establishment.[10]

Gussow and Tracy took the position that self-help groups represent a significant consumer response to a basic inadequacy in classical adaptation and rehabilitation.[11]

Expressive/social influence group. Self-help groups can also be seen within the familiar expressive/instrumental, expressive/social influence frame of reference. Killilea suggested:

> Groups which can be classified primarily as expressive are concerned principally with the self-interest and satisfaction of their members (i.e., A.A. and Synanon). Instrumental groups seek primarily to influence the larger society and to bring about change on behalf of the interests of their members (i.e., homophile organizations which focus on combating discrimination in employment, housing and the media.)[12]

A vehicle to aid in coping with life-cycle transitions. Self-help programs can also provide new roles for the participants. In her analysis of services provided in a widow-to-widow mutual-help program, Abrahams found that the dynamics of mutual aid constantly evolve, allowing both helper and recipient to adapt to new roles and find new opportunities for healthy personal growth: "This mutual help service among the widowed involved a two-way helping process in which both sides met needs and derived satisfactions. The volunteers who became helpers were greatly helped in their own adjustment process."[13]

Similarly, the self-help activities reported in this study permit the elderly to serve others and, at the same time, fulfill their own needs.

HISTORICAL PERSPECTIVE OF
SELF-HELP GROUPS

Self-help groups were organized as early as the 1800s. However, only in the past eighty-four years have self-help groups developed into a cohesive response to shared social, emotional, physical, and economic conditions.[14]

Katz and Bender identified extra-familial groups during the Industrial Revolution and friendly societies in late nineteenth-century England as the historical beginnings of self-help groups.[15] Other writers discussed the conditions out of which self-help groups arose such as industrialization, a money economy, and the growth of big business, industry and government. These conditions in turn led to:

1. depersonalization and dehumanization of institutions and social life;

2. feelings of alienation and powerlessness;

3. the sense, for many people, that they were unable to control the events that shaped their lives;

4. loss of choices;

5. feelings of being trapped by impersonal forces;

6. decline of the sense of community and identity, compounded for many by the loss of belief in church, state, progress, political parties and other established institutions and values; and the

7. erosion of the traditional family structure.

One should note too that as early as 1896 parents' association groups were organized to sponsor lectures concerned with common problems of parents and attempt to foster cooperation with teachers.[16] Later, during the 1930s the self-help group movement experienced rapid growth in response to the worldwide Depression. Barish indicated that self-help groups were established in California in the 1930s to combat unemployment through unemployment cooperatives, and that in 1936 former concentration-camp victims formed self-help groups to aid newcomers with jobs, advice and emotional support.[17] In the late 1930s self-help groups expanded to include people with physical and emotional disabilities. Parents of handicapped children eventually merged into the American Association for Retarded Children; the United Cerebral Palsy Foundation also developed during this period. In 1937, Abraham Low, a Chicago psychiatrist, led the formation of Recovery, Inc., the first self-help group for mental patients.

Barish asserts that one of the most important self-help groups formed during the 1930s was Alcoholic Anonymous. Frank Buchman, a Lutheran minister, organized the Oxford group, later called Moral Rearmament. A.A. was started in Akron, Ohio, in 1933 by two former members of the Oxford group. By 1939, the Akron group[18] had one hundred members.

By 1977, there were over 500,000 self-help groups, according to Gartner and Riessman. Among the largest were the National Association for Retarded Children with over 1,300 local units and more than 130,000 members by 1970,[19] and Alcoholic Anonymous, which had 30,000 chapters in 192 countries in 1978.[20] Gartner and Riessman also pointed out that in a two county area of New York State A.A., Al-Anon, Gamblers Anonymous, Gam-Anon, Overeaters Anonymous and Tops had more than 180 groups and a self-help group existed to combat nearly every major disease listed by the World Health Organization.[21]

During the late 1960s, several researchers examined self-help and mutual-aid programs for the elderly. More recently, research on self-help groups for the elderly has grown rapidly. For example, Sherman found that mutual assistance was virtually nonexistent among elderly neighbors.[22]

In her study of older Blacks in Chicago, Lopata discovered that contacts and interaction of the elderly with friends, neighbors, and children were at best, sporadic.[23] However, Taylor reported a different point of view based on results of his research while he was a research fellow with the "Program for Research on Black Americans" at the Institute for Social Research, University of Michigan. Respondents in his sample reported frequent interaction with family members, relatively close residential proximity to immediate family and relatives, and extensive familial affective bonds."[24] Other researchers, including Faulkner and Heisel, Cantor, and Litwak et al. have found that there is an extensive self-help/mutual support network operating among the elderly and their children, friends, neighbors, and significant others.[25] In fact, recent reports have asserted that the family provides the majority of care to the elderly.[26] The bulk of the organized literature on self-help, especially as reviewed by Gartner and Riessman, Caplan and Killilea, and Lieberman and Borman,[27] have focused on the more formal self-help groups such as support groups for mental patients, alcoholics, physically disabled, etc. These groups were developed to help the participants gain back a more improved level of health and more stabilized functional condition. There is another stream of literature (e.g., Wentowski),[28] which has centered on the more spontaneous and/or formal types of support and interactions existing between the elderly and their neighbors and friends. They may not be ill but simply need the involvement of a network to help compensate for their personal limitations. This study leans in the latter direction.

SELF-HELP GROUPS VERSUS FORMAL ORGANIZATIONS

The advantages and disadvantages of self-help groups for the elderly can be discussed on three levels: (1) advantages of self-help groups mediating between the individual and the formal organization; (2) the advantages of self-help to the individual participants; and (3) disadvantages of self-help groups for the individual participants. Let us examine these three categories.

Mediating Between the Individual and the Formal Organization

Many positive features characterize self-help activities. Among these are self-help groups which emphasize the concrete, the subjective, the experimental and the intuitive in contrast to reflective, systematic knowledge and understanding that is the premise of professional help.

Katz and Bender noted that the unique quality of human service is that much of the work can be performed by people with no formal systematic knowledge or training; rather, their abilities and skills rest on their humanness, feeling for people, caring, down-to-earth experience and common sense, spontaneity, availability, and time. This description, of course, is applicable to most self-help groups and their individual members.

Some writers believe that self-help groups have grown, in large measure, because of the unwillingness and/or inability of formal organizations to resolve many of the social service problems of these groups. Such formal organizations often are perceived as having an overly intellectualized orientation, requiring excessive credentialism and possessing limited reach in regard to various populations.[29]

Therefore, the advantages of self-help when the individual interfaces with formal organizations are that the self-help group: (1) represents an important advance in human service technology; (2) is usually categorized as a growth-promoting, helpful support system; (3) provides a challenge to the professional; (4) complements or supplements professional services; (5) provides an alternative to professional help; and (6) expands and enriches professional practice.[30]

Advantages of Self-Help to the Individual

One of the important functions of self-help groups is to aid members in finding workable approaches to many personal dilemmas. The self-help groups attempt to do this through: (1) developing and sustaining a coherent view of the world and the member's place in it; (2) helping the member learn new and more gratifying behavior; (3) helping the member tap his unconscious feelings; (4) fortifying the members self-image and pride; (5) helping the member achieve environmental mastery by uncovering or discovering his competence and by using the competence of each member to the fullest; (6) increasing the individual's coping abilities through his participation in group tasks of graduated difficulty; and (7) advancing the member to new levels of self-perception and status within the group toward the time when he feels ready to leave it.[31] Most of these functions are applicable to older people.

Disadvantages of Self-Help to the Individual

Some of the disadvantages of the self-help groups, as pointed out by these writers, were that self-help groups: (1) are seen as agencies of social control which may have some repressive features that are psychologically and sociopolitically undesirable; (2) members over-identify with each other, have uncontrolled subjectivity, and in some cases, inadequate knowledge that can seriously limit the value of the care they provide; (3) foster lifelong dependence for some of the users; (4) lead to an exacerbation of resources and power; and (5) have a tendency to blame the victim rather than changing the victimizing circumstances. These writers suggested that since the groups cannot replace the expertise provided by professionals in situations where technical skills are required, the self-help groups should educate professionals to work more humanely with their patients and clients.

Other writers, including Lieberman and Borman, have suggested the exchange theory as a base for examining the interactions which occur in self-help groups:

> For those seeking help as well as those offering help, the exchange of tangible and intangible resources provides a framework for examining the helping process as well as the pathways through which individuals locate necessary resources. Individuals may seek out self-help not because they are disappointed users of their societal resources nor because other resources are unavailable but rather because self-help groups require the least expenditure of resources and the least effort in order to locate a needed resource for themselves.[32]

THE EXCHANGE THEORY CONCEPT

The exchange theory is the conceptual basis for the present study. Close attention will be paid to Dowd's adaptation of exchange theory to social gerontology. In his reelaboration of the theory, Dowd drew upon " the later development of exchange theory which details the nexus between exchange and power in order to reconceptualize the relationship between age and social structure as a process of exchange."[33]

Hess discussed the importance of support systems and self-help, stating that "Old may be defined as a period of decreasing involvement in networks, i.e., family, neighborhood, and work relationships whether voluntary or not. Situations that may have been firm anchors in past decades are no longer so secure for any of us, but especially for the old."[34]

With the absence of elderly people's involvement in the networks described above, or the unavailability of anchors in society for them, Hess suggested that two possible conditions are generated. First, behavior or attitude adaptations are created which reduce strain and bring capacities into consonance with available roles, or, second, new roles are created to meet personal and group needs. She further suggested that self-help groups are model vehicles for creating new order and meaning in elderly people's lives.[35]

The exchange theory suggests a central concern with reciprocity, logically among equals whether in terms of equal resources or equal deprivation. While relatives would be the logical first source of support for the elderly, Hess revealed that most studies show that fully 20 percent of elderly respondents reported not having one child living close enough for frequent contact while an additional one fourth to one third did not have living children. These individuals relied on friends and neighbors for primary support. She indicated, however, that there was little evidence that old people increased interaction with one another to compensate for the reduced level of family interaction. What seemed to occur most of the time was that older people continued to maintain the life-style to which they had become accustomed during earlier years. In essence, some older people had high levels of interaction with both kin and neighbors while others maintained consistently lower levels of contact with all support sources.[36]

There were contrasting views on this issue. Sherman reported on a survey of six retirement housing sites in California. The surveyors found no overall greater assistance given by neighbors than by children.[37] In her study of older Black widows in a Chicago community, Lopata also found that contacts and interactions with friends, neighbors, siblings, children and other kin were, at best, sporadic throughout widowhood.[38] However, a more recent review of pertinent studies provided evidence that the family was, in fact, the major provider of care to the elderly.[39] In addition to the help given by family members, researcher have shown that friends and neighbors are part of the support network for the elderly. For example, Faulkner found in a Newark, New Jersey study that the "support network was undeniably based upon a foundation of interaction with friends and neighbors.[40] She also found that two thirds of the respondents helped friends and neighbors and another fifth was involved with friends as often as family. Cantor, in reporting on her study of the inner-city elderly, stated that:

> Although a city like New York has a myriad of voluntary and governmental agencies ready to provide assistance to citizens in need, turning to such agencies is far from the first reaction of most residents including the elderly. Older Americans are fiercely independent and desirous of managing on their own, or if necessary turning to those with whom they have primary relationship such as child or neighbor.[41]

In addition, Wentowski provided empirical data on the use and impact of reciprocity in the exchange system as the elderly interact in the support network. Her data were derived from a participant-observer study of fifty older adults over a two-year period in a relatively large city in the Southeastern United States. A major focus of the study was to "Find out the actual dynamics of how participants in the support networks defined the performances and behavior they expected of one another, and how they determined who was eligible to become a part of the networks."[42]

Wentowski's report focused on two main themes: the cultural rules governing the reciprocal exchanges; and "balanced reciprocity." She reported that "basic to the cultural rule governing reciprocity is that something received requires something returned."[43] When an elderly person accepted an offer of help within a face-to face context, he or she was, in essence, obligated to the giver. The acceptance also indicated a willingness by the receiver to make a commitment to the giver.

The "balanced reciprocity" theme helped to define the relationship whether between kin or non-kin. It referred to "exchanges in which an equivalent of the thing received is returned within a finite time period."[44] Wentowski discussed two types of exchanges that were based on the balanced-reciprocity theme. Immediate exchange was used between two persons who wished to keep the obligation at a minimum-- repayment was made at once in the exact equivalent of what was received; this exchange was usually referred to as instrumental exchange. Deferred exchange was used when the person wished to extend the relationship--it tended to express a willingness to trust and to assume greater obligation. When a gift or service was given, time was permitted to elapse before payment was expected. This type of exchange was reportedly effective in establishing new relationships between non-kin such as friends and neighbors.[45]

Wentowski supports the position others have taken that kin are expected to be the most consistent helpers. In fact, her study found that a majority of the people relied heavily on one or more kin-persons. It also found that distant kin and non-kin were, at times, substituted when close kin were unavailable or unresponsive. Thus, one might reasonably conclude that the literature provides clear evidence of informal exchange systems among the elderly.

Dowd stated that theoretical concerns within social gerontology have revolved mostly around theories of disengagement and activity and suggested that the "disengagement/activity paradigm" should be put aside at least temporarily in order to enlarge the field of alternative perspectives on adult development.[46] He further pointed out that previous attempts at theory construction in social gerontology have not succeeded because of the failure to recognize that decreased social interaction in old age is a result not only of the conditions of widowhood, poor health, and lowered income, but also of an intricate exchange process between society and the aged resulting from their power-dependent relationships.[47] Before discussing Dowd's adaptation of exchange theory to social gerontology, a review of the basic concept is appropriate.

Several social theory analysts--using the assumption that organizations can best be studied through analysis of the interactions among their members--developed the guiding principles of exchange theory.[48] The views of these theorists were summarized by J. Eugene Haas and Thomas E. Drabek.[49]

First, they presented the objective description and analysis patterns of interactions developed from the work of Chapple; then they charted the work of C.I. Barnard and William Foote Whyte. Haas and Drabek also indicated that Homans, by extracting from the work of Whyte and others (including the influence of behavioral psychologists like B.F. Skinner), constructed a theoretical model for exchange theory. Homan's basic concept encompassed interaction as an exchange relationship between two or more persons. He also described social behavior as a tangible or intangible exchange of activity between people that was more or less rewarding or costly. In these exchange relationships, certain forms of each person's behavior are reinforced to some degree by the behavior of others, and each person finds certain behavior patterns of others reinforcing.[50]

Alvin Gouldner, also wary of the abstract formulations of organizational interactions as developed by natural systems theorists, developed the concept of "reciprocity." He stressed reciprocity as an important part of exchange, describing it as "the pattern of exchange through which the mutual dependence of people brought about by the division of labor is realized."[51]

In summarizing the models of the exchange theorists, Haas and Drabek listed nine central ideas which embraced the core of the theorists' viewpoint:

1. Analytical focus should be on persons and their interactions--one should first seek to describe the

structure or pattern of observed interaction. In order to clearly understand the process of decision-making in an interactional process, one must understand what people are included in the process of providing information, what people give advice, what people are involved in the discussion of a given decision.

2. Interaction patterns can be observed and measured in a rigorous and objective fashion. This can be done through the careful counting of the frequency and duration of member interactions.

3. Member interactions, once observed, can be analyzed at several different levels: (a) the level of individual personality; (b) the interaction systems (group) may be the unit of analysis; and (c) organizations may be the unit of analysis. It may also serve as a basis for analysis of the interfacing between these levels.

4. Member interaction may also be analyzed at a transactional level. At this level, collection of observed interactions are grouped into even sequences of different types. These events which involved the giving-receiving of rewards or penalties may be of seven levels: (a) positive exchange; (b) trading; (c) joint payoff; (d) competitive; (e) negative exchange; (f) open conflict; and (g) bargaining.

5. Many patterns of interaction may be explained through analysis of exchange transaction--a brief summary of Blau's analysis of this process is that exchange transactions often produce differentiation in power because of the imbalance of obligations incurred. Power may be gained by providing services desired by others who become dependent on the supplier. General approval of such power legitimate it, and the relationship may become stabilized as long as the exchange rate is viewed as "fair."

6. Exchange processes that characterize relationships among persons in small groups have counterparts in more complex systems, but there are important differences for many of the transactions are indirect rather than face-to-face.

7. As interaction patterns persist over time, interpersonal relationships emerge. Therefore, it is important to understand the composition of the interpersonal relations among all of the group members as well as the composite sentiments of all the individuals.

8. Groups and organizations maintain stability through a system of norms and sanctions. Individuals enter groups with expectations based on their prior experiences about how persons in various social positions ought to behave. Thus, a series of interlocking roles or groups of expectations emerge that structure future interaction, thereby making it increasingly patterned.

9. To what degree does the exchange perspective have utility for analysis of social behavior in places other than the United States? All of the theorists expressed the hope that they were generating a perspective that would be useful in cross cultural analysis.[52]

After summarizing the theorists' ideas, Haas and Drabek presented six major criticisms:

1. Too often the distinctions between normative and interpersonal expectations are blurred. Usually the normative expectations being discussed become expectations associated with particular persons rather than with social positions;

2. Despite the statements regarding distinctive levels of analysis, efforts to "humanize" the research often result in reductionist strategies. While interaction patterns are noted and defined, the source of explanation tends very often to end up focusing on the personality of the actor;

3. Except in Blau's work, conflict is too often viewed as necessarily undesirable behavior that is to be resolved through better human relations;

4. Masses of data are collected, but movement toward generalizations occur too seldom;

5. Those working within the human relations perspective have too often ignored the formal structure of organizations as a set of variables that might be used to account for observed behavior patterns; and

6. Little effort has been made to analyze or conceptualize environmental influences or organizational environment interactions.[53]

Although initially formulated in relation to organizational transactions, the exchange theory also provided an alternative perspective for analyzing the social processes of aging with those supplied by the disengagement and activity theorists. A basic assumption underlying much exchange-theory research is that interaction between individuals or collectives can be characterized as, according to Dowd, "attempts to maximize rewards and reduce costs."[54]

Certain patterns of interaction among social actors are sustained over time because people, for whatever reason, find such interaction rewarding. In seeking rewards, however, costs are inevitably incurred involving the negative value or unpleasantness experienced in the course of obtaining a reward or involving the positive value associated with an alternative course or action forsaken to pursue the chosen rewarding activity.

Dowd further pointed out that a major tenet of exchange theory is that interaction between two or more social actors will most probably be continued and positively evaluated if the actors "profit from the interaction and that the variable of power enters the analysis of exchange theory when one of the participants in the exchange values the rewards gained in the relationship more than the other."[55]

The basic thrust of exchange theory, as discussed by Dowd, emphasizes the concept of an exchange of more or less rewarding actions between two or more social actors with the notion of power as a critical factor. The partner in a social exchange who depends less on the exchange for gratification has a power advantage which can be used to command compliance from the exchange partner.

In discussing the use of the exchange support network in creating support for the elderly, Wentowski suggested that: The amount of support received in old age varies according to many factors beyond most people's control, such as available material and financial resources and number of close kin living nearby. However, the quality of support during old age is contingent on the quality of relationship over time. Lacking the longevity of exchange pattern, some people buy into the system of generalized reciprocity by making very large gifts for which no immediate returns are expected.[56]

In the case of the aged, there is a series of exchange relationships where the relative power of the aged, vis-a-vis their social environment, is diminished to the point that the basic aspect of their interaction is that of compliance. Thus, the exchange theory suggests that the degree of engagement in old age is a factor of a specific exchange relationship between an individual or group of individuals as well as the society in which the more powerful exchange partner dictates the terms of the relationship.[57] Faulkner et al. also found that the givers in the exchange relationship had greater acceptance of their life situation and scored higher on the positive-relationship-to-enjoyment-of-life-aspects as opposed to receivers.[58] Dowd, in *Stratification Among the Aged*, argued that the status of old people can improve providing they continue their engagement in the exchange network. This is because exchange relations tends toward balance; but in order for the balanced state to evolve, the exchange relationship must endure. Older people must engage themselves in the course of their everyday social interactions.[59]

In view of the above, it is therefore suggested in this study that self-help activities may be used as a means to strengthen or compensate for the diminishing power base of the elderly.

Now that the literature relating to self-help groups in general and self-help groups for the elderly in particular has been explored, let us turn to Chapter III, "Research Design and Methodology."

Notes

1. National Association of Social Workers, *Encyclopedia of Social Work*, Sixteenth Issue, Volume, 1973, 1165.

2. In the literature, one will find a number of terms to describe self-help (i.e., mutual aid, support network, informal support network, mutual support, etc.). They will be used interchangeably in this study.

3. Alfred H. Katz and Eugene I. Bender, *The Strength in Us: Self-Help Groups in the Modern World* (New York: New Viewpoint, a Division of Franklin Watts, 1976); Alan Gartner and Frank Riessman, *Self-help in the Human Services* (San Francisco: Jossey-Bass, Inc., Publishers, 1977); Leonard D. Borman et al., eds., "Helping People to Help Themselves: Self-Help and Prevention," in *The Prevention in Human Services* (New York: The Haworth Press, 1982), vol 1, no 3; and Morton A. Lieberman and Leonard D. Borman and Associates, *Self-Help Groups for Coping With Crisis* (San Francisco: Jossey-Bass Publishers, 1979).

4. M. Joanna Mellor, Harriet Rzetelny, and Iris Hudis, "Self-Help Groups for Caregivers of the Aged", in *The Self-Help Revolution*, ed. Alan Gartner and Frank Riessman (New York: Human Sciences Press, Inc., 1984).

5. Katz and Bender, *The Strength in Us*, 3.

6. Gartner and Riessman, *Self-Help in the Human Services*, 9.

7. Maria Killilea, "Mutual Help Organizations: Interpretations in the Literature," in *Support Systems and Mutual Help: Multidisciplinary Explorations*, ed. Gerald Caplan and Maria Killilea (New York: Grune and Straton, Inc., 1976), 37-38.

8. Ibid., 41-63.

9. Ibid., 41.

10. Donald M. Traunstein and Richard Steinman, "Voluntary Self-Help Organizations: An Exploratory Study," *Journal of Voluntary Action Research*, 4 (1973): 230-239.

11. Zachary Gussow and George S. Tracy, "The Role of Self-Help Groups in Adaptation to Chronic Illness and Disability," *Journal of Social Science and Medicine*, 10, no. 7/8 (1976): 407-414.

12. Killilea, "Mutual Help Organizations," 59-60.

13. Ruby Banks Abrahams, "Mutual Help for the Widowed," *Social Work*, 17, no. 5 (September 1972): 54-61.

14. *Encyclopedia of Social Work*, Sixteenth Issue, vol.II, "Self-Help Groups," by Herbert Barish, 1163-1168.

15. Katz and Bender, *The Strength in Us*, 5.

16. Barish, "Self-Help Groups," 1165.

17. Ibid.

18. Ibid.

19. Gartner and Riessman, *Self-Help in the Human Services*, 6.

20. Lieberman and Borman, *Self-Help Groups for Coping with Crisis*, 32.

21. Gartner and Riessman, *The Self-Help Revolution*, 7.

22. Susan R. Sherman, "Mutual Assistance and Support in Retirement Housing," *Journal of Gerontology*, 30, no. 4 (1975): 479-483.

23. Helen Z. Lopata, "Social Relations of Widows in Black and White Urban Communities," in *Social and Family Relations of Black Widows in Urban Communities* (U.S. Department of Health, Education,

and Welfare, Social Rehabilitation Service, 1965; unpublished research, Administration on Aging).

24. Robert Joseph Taylor, "Receipt of Support from Family Among Black Americans: Demographic and Familial Differences," *Journal of Marriage and the Family*, 48 (February 1986): 67-77.

25. Audrey O Faulkner and Marcel A Heisel, "Giving, Receiving, and Exchanging: Elderly Blacks and Their Informal Support Systems" (a paper presented at the 30th Annual Meeting of the Gerontological Society, 1977); Marjorie H. Cantor, "The Formal and Informal Social Support System of Older New Yorkers" (paper presented at the 10th International Congress of Gerontology, Jerusalem, Israel, June 1975); Eugene Litwak, in collaboration with John Dono, Cecilia Falbe, Barbara Kail, Steve Kulis, Sam Marullo, and Roger Sherman, *The Modified Extended Family, Social Networks, and Research Continuities in Aging*, Monograph 73, 1981 (prepared for a University Seminar, Duke University, Durham, North Carolina).

26. *Family Caregiving and the Elderly: Policy Recommendations and Research Findings* (New York State Office for the Aging, March 1983); Alan M. Jette, S.L. Tennstedt, and L.G. Branch, "Stability of Informal Long-Term Care," *Journal of Aging and Health*, 4, no. 2 (1992): 193-211; and M.J. Armstrong and K. S. Goldsteen, "Friendship Support Patterns of Older American Women", *Journal of Aging Studies*, 4, no 4 (1990): 391-404.

27. Gartner and Riessman, *Self-Help in the Human Services* and *The Self-Help Revolution*; Caplan and Killilea, *Support Systems and Mutual Help: Multidisciplinary Explorations*; and Lieberman and Borman, *Self-Help Groups for Coping with Crisis*.

28. Gloria J. Wentowski, "Reciprocity and the Coping Strategies of Older People: Cultural Dimensions of Network Building," *The Gerontologist*, 21, no 6 (1987).

29. Katz and Bender, *The Strength in Us*, 5.

30. Gartner and Riessman, *Self-Help in the Human Services*, 9-10; Katz and Bender, *The Strength in Us*, 108-109; and Victor W. Sidel and Ruth Sidel, "Beyond Coping," *Social Policy*, September/October 1976, 67-69.

31. The above list of functions of self-help groups was developed by Katz and Bender, *The Strength in Us*, 108-109.

32. Lieberman and Borman, *Self-Help Groups for Coping with Crisis*, 117.

33. James J. Dowd, "Aging as Exchange: A Preface Theory," *Journal of Gerontology*, 30, no. 5 (1975): 584-594.

34. Beth Hess, "Self-Help Among the Aged," *Social Policy*, 7, no. 3 (November/December 1976): 55.

35. Ibid.

36. Ibid., 57.

37. Susan R. Sherman, "Mutual Assistance and Support in Retirement Housing," *Journal of Gerontology*, 30, no. 4 (1975): 479-483.

38. Helen Z. Lopata, "Social Relations of Widows in Black and White Urban Communities," in *Social and Family Relations of Black Widows in Urban Communities* (U.S. Department of Health, Education, and Welfare, Social Rehabilitation Service, 1965; unpublished research, Administration on Aging).

39. New York State Office for the Aging, *Family Caregiving and the Elderly; Policy Recommendations and Research Findings*, March 1983.

40. Faulkner and Heisel, "Giving, Receiving, and Exchanging," 4.

41. Cantor, "The Formal and Informal Social Support System of Older New Yorkers," 13.

42. Wentowski, "Reciprocity and the Coping Strategies of Older People," 601.

43. Ibid., 603.

44. Ibid., 603.

45. Ibid., 604.

46. Dowd, "Aging as Exchange," 584.

47. Ibid., 585.

48. The Social Theory Analysts included: Eliot D. Chapple, "Measuring Human Relations: An Introduction to the Study of the Interaction of Individuals," *Genetic Psychology Monographs*, 22 no. 60 (1940); George C. Homans, "Social Behavior as Exchange," *American Journal of Sociology*, 62, no. 597 (May 1958); Peter M. Blau, *Exchange and Power in Social Life* (New York: John Wiley and Sons, Inc., 1964); Chester I. Bernard, *The Functions of the Executives* (Cambridge: Harvard University Press, 1938); William F. Whyte, *Street Corner Society* (Chicago: University of Chicago Press, 1943; Alvin W. Gouldner," The Norm of Reciprocity: A Preliminary Statement," *American Sociological Review*, 24, no. 163 (April 1960).

49. J. Eugene Haas and Thomas E. Drabek, *Complex Organizations a Sociological Perspective* (New York: MacMillan Publishing Company, Inc., 1973), 60-72.

50. Ibid., 63.

51. Ibid., 64.

52. Ibid., 64-69.

53. Ibid., 72.

54. Dowd, "Aging as Exchange," 586.

55. Ibid., 593.

56. Wentowski, "Reciprocity and the Coping Strategies of Older People," 605.

57. Dowd, "Aging as Exchange," 593.

58. Faulkner and Heisel, "Giving, Receiving, and Exchanging," 6.

59. James J. Dowd, *Stratification Among the Aged* (Monterey, CA: Brooks/Cole Publication Company, a Division of Wadsworth, Iinc., 1980), 122-123.

III
RESEARCH DESIGN AND METHODOLOGY

The goal of the present study, conducted at two social activity centers for the aged in New York City, was to gather descriptive information about the self-help activities engaged in by the participants at the two centers as well as information regarding the mutual support between them and their relatives, friends, and neighbors. The study included interviews of forty-eight[1] senior citizens who were selected from among those registered at the two centers.

RESEARCH QUESTIONS

In the context of the goal stated above, the following research questions were part of the study:

1. What was the relationship between help received from friends and demographic characteristics of the respondents (*e.g.*, age, sex, family status, ethnicity, and education)?

2. What was the relationship between help received from friends and (a) number of living children; (b) interaction with children; (c) interaction with siblings; (d) interaction with relatives; (e) mobility; (f) use of social services; and (g) interaction with formal non-senior citizens' social group participation?

3. What was the relationship between help received from children and demographic characteristics of the respondents?

31

4. What was the relationship between help received from children and (a) number of living children; (b) interaction with children; (c) interaction with siblings; (d) interaction with relatives; (e) mobility; (f) use of social services; and (g) interaction with formal non-senior citizens social group participation?

5. What was the relationship between help given to children by respondents and demographic characteristics of the respondents?

6. What was the relationship between help given to children by respondents and (a) number of living children; (b) interaction with children; (c) interaction with siblings; (d) interaction with relatives; (e) mobility; (f) use of social services; and (g) interaction with formal non-senior citizens' social group participation?

7. What was the relationship between patterns of escort services for the elderly and demographic characteristics of the respondents?

8. What was the relationship between patterns of escort services for the elderly and (a) number of living children; (b) interaction with children; (c) interaction with siblings; (d) interaction with relatives; (e) mobility; (f) use of social services; and (g) interaction with formal non-senior citizens' social group participation?

9. What was the relationship between the perception of helping sources and demographic characteristics of the respondents?

10. What was the relationship between (a) perception; (b) interaction with children; (c) interaction with siblings; (d) interaction with relatives; (e) mobility; (f) use of social services; and (g) interaction with formal non-senior citizens' social group participation?

11. What was the correlation between different self-help activities?

Chapter III discusses the study sample, the operationalization of the study variables and data collection procedures.

THE SAMPLE

The subjects interviewed in this study were forty-eight senior citizens registered at two social activity centers in New York City. One center was in a relatively secluded development located in Far Rockaway, New York, which housed only senior citizens. The total population for this development was approximately 1,300 residents living in 900 units. Twenty-three percent of the residents ranged in age between 62 and 72; 76 percent were 72 years of age or over; 80 percent were female; 80 percent were single and 20 percent were married; 85 percent were white and 15 percent were Black. The average length of stay in the development was five to six years. All of the residents were automatically registered at the social activity center and came into contact with the staff whether or not they participated in the social activities of the center.

The second social activity center was located in a housing development of approximately 4,200 residents in a relatively diverse area (in terms of ethnic background and age) of the Marble Hill section of the West Bronx. The demographics of the housing development were as follows: youth under 25, 37 percent; adults 62 years of age and over, 17 percent; the remaining 46 percent were between the ages of 25 and 62. Fifty-nine percent of the residents were Black, 23 percent Puerto Rican, 1.7 percent white, and 6 percent other. The average income was $12,805 and the average length of time living in the development was 13.2 years. People from the surrounding community participated in the social activity center as well, which accounted for the larger number of whites participating in the center's activities; the center had approximately 2,500 people registered with an average daily attendance of 140.

These two social activity centers were operated under the auspices of the Associated Young Men and Women's Hebrew Association of Greater New York (YM/YWHA) and were chosen as the study site for the following reasons: (1) the sponsoring agency for these programs, the Associated Young Men and Women's Hebrew Association of Greater New York (frequently referred to as Associated Y's) was interested in developing a profile of the residents who participated in the activities of these two centers; (2) the support and assistance of the staff of both centers was pledged in the collection of the data; and (3) both centers had among their registrants large numbers of elderly persons who were likely to be participants in self-help activities.

Initially, a systematic random selection of 35 subjects from among the registered members of each center was made. An alphabetized system of registration cards was maintained in each center. From these cards, starting with member number 1 in each center, every twentieth member was selected until a pool of 35 subjects was drawn--a total of 70 subjects from the two centers. In Center 1, three subjects decided, after the initiation of the interview, not to participate, leaving 32 subjects. In Center 2, once the interview began, five subjects decided not to participate. Of the remaining 30 subjects, three completed less than half of the interview schedule at the initial interview, but agreed to a follow-up interview. However, it proved impossible to complete these interviews due to difficulty in arranging a mutually convenient time with the subjects, leaving 27 completed interviews from Center 2. In addition, individual interviews having incomplete or missing data on more than 10 percent of the items were dropped, leaving 48 subjects.

Table 1 shows the demographic characteristics of the sample population. With respect to age as seen above, at the time of the interview 39 percent of the subjects were between 60 and 70 years old, 41 percent were between the ages of 71 and 75, while the remaining 19 percent were 76 years and over. A majority of the subjects, 81 percent, were either single, divorced, or widowed, while only 19 percent were still married. Females represented 90 percent of the sample and almost three-fourths, 73 percent, of the subjects were Jewish. The non-Jewish population, 27 percent, included Blacks, Irish, Italians and others. Slightly fewer than half of the subjects were without a high school diploma (27 percent had 8 years of schooling or less, and 21 percent had 9 to 11 years of school), and the remainder of the subjects were high school graduates (36 percent had high school diplomas and 15 percent had post-high school education). Twenty-nine percent of the sample lived on incomes of $3,999 or less; 31 percent had incomes of between $4,000 and $7,999; 17 percent had incomes of $8,000 plus. However, 23 percent of the sample gave no response to the income question. The typical respondent could be described as a Jewish female, between the ages of 71 and 75 who was not married and one-half possessed at least a high school education.

Study Limitations

Several considerations limited the generalizability of these findings. First, the Far Rockaway housing development operated under Section 8 regulations (one of the eligibility requirements being limited income). During the period of data collection, the residents' income was under review. During the pre-interview meeting with residents, a frequently expressed concern was that the interviews would expose their income.

Table 1
Frequencies for Socio-Demographic Characteristics

	Number	*Percent*
Age Groups		
60-70	19	38.8
71-75	20	40.8
76 years and over	9	18.4
Total	48	100.0
Marital Status		
Single (separated, divorced, widowed)	38	80.9
Married	9	19.1
Missing	1	0.0
Total	48	100.0
Sex		
Male	5	10.4
Female	43	89.6
Total	48	100.0
Ethnicity		
Jewish	35	72.9
Non-Jewish	13	27.1
Total	48	100.0
Education		
8 years or less	13	27.1
9 to 11 years	10	20.8
High school diploma	18	37.5
Post-high school	7	14.6
Total		
Income		
$3,999 or less	14	29.2
$4,000 to $7,999	15	31.3
$8,000 plus	8	16.7
Missing	11	22.9
Total	48	100.0

Even though efforts were made to dispel this concern, the fact that 23 percent of the final 48 subjects had missing income data suggests apprehension. The researcher was not aware of the income review until after the interviews had been arranged.

Second, two other factors may have colored the responses of the subjects: (1) the director of Center 1 contacted the selected subjects and brought them together as a group prior to the interviews. This could have adversely affected the preference of some subjects to remain anonymous and thus may have biased their responses; and (2) 81 percent of the subjects in Center 1 were interviewed by their peers (two member volunteers). This could have affected the information received, because the subjects may have been reluctant to share personal information about themselves and their family such as income status or, in some instances, their relationships with their children. That 19 percent of the subjects preferred to be interviewed by someone unfamiliar to them supports this assumption. However, the method of data collection in Center 1 was suggested by the center director and supported by the membership associations president. Approval from both was required in order to conduct the survey.

Yet another possible factor, existing in Center 2, was that it operated a full lunch program sponsored with funds from Title 7 of the Nutrition Act. Many of the subjects visited the center only for that purpose rather than for other activities or supportive relationships. Other facts which limited the study were the small number of subjects interviewed, and only two locations used for interviews, requiring that many of the responses to questions be collapsed in order to make them meaningful.

SPECIFICATION OF THE STUDY VARIABLES

The independent variables in the study related to: (1) the demographic characteristics of the subject (e.g., age, marital status, sex, ethnicity, and education); (2) the subjects' interaction with their families; (3) the mobility of the subjects in their daily life activities; (4) the social service agencies in which they were involved; and (5) the formal non-senior citizens' social group participation of the subjects. Each of these independent variables was broken down as follows:

A. Demographic Variables
   (1) age, (2) family status, (3) sex, (4) ethnicity, and (5) education.
B. Family Related Variables
   (1) number of living children;
   (2) number of children living in the metropolitan New York area;
   (3) number of children seen monthly or more;
   (4) number of children with telephone contact at least weekly;
   (5) number of siblings living in metropolitan New York area; and
   (6) number of relatives living in the metropolitan New York area.
C. Mobility Variables--these included counts of the Places subjects traveled:
   (1) ten blocks or less to visit;
   (2) more than ten blocks to visit;
   (3) on foot to visit;
   (4) by public transportation to visit;
   (5) by private transportation to visit.
D. Social Service Agency Variables
   (1) the subjects use or non-use of social service agencies;
   (2) a count of the number of situations when the subjects perceived the formal agency personnel as the major helping source;
   (3) number of social agencies the subjects turned to for help.
E. Formal Non-Senior Citizens' Social Group Participation
   (1) the subjects' visits to religious organizations;
   (2) the subjects' visits to other organizations;
   (3) total number of groups the subjects visited;
   (4) the subjects' visits to similar groups in earlier life.

The dependent variables of this study related to the self-help activities in which the subjects engaged on a daily basis. Also examined was the mutual support exchanged between the subjects and their families, friends and neighbors under various circumstances, including short-term crises, long-term crises and social and recreational interaction. These dependent variables were listed as follows:

A. Escort functions of the self-help group:
   (1) a count of the places to which the subjects *don't go* in the course of daily life tasks;
   (2) a count of the places to which the subjects *go alone*;
   (3) a count of the places to which the subjects *go with family;*
   (4) a count of the places to which the subjects *go with friends.*
B. Help received from friends scale (*e.g.*, visits with each other, running errands, providing conversation, helping out during illness, going on trips together, support in times of crisis).
C. Independent items from the help received from friends scale:
   (1) friends give you advice on money matters;
   (2) friends help you make a decision on a big purchase;
   (3) friends give you gifts.
D. Help received from children scale (*e.g.*, help in time of illness, with advice on money matters, with decision regarding a big purchase, with shopping and/or running errands, giving gifts, repairs around the house, housekeeping chores, preparing of meals, taking respondents on trips, serving as escort for respondent).
E. Independent item from the help received from children scale: Children help you out with money.
F. Help given to children by the elderly scale (*e.g.*, help out in time of illness, shop or run errands, give gifts, help out with money, repairs around the house, give advice on money matters, help with decision-making when purchasing a big item, housekeeping).
G. Independent items from the help given to children by the elderly scale:
   (1) Babysit with grandchildren;
   (2) Elderly give advice on running the home and bringing up grandchildren.
H. Perceptions of helping sources:
   (1) count of the number of situations in which subjects perceived self as the major helping source;
   (2) count of the number of situations in which subjects perceived relatives as the major helping source; and
   (3) count of the number of situations in which subjects perceived friends as the major helping source.

I. Visits a group of friends: whether or not the subjects participated in a group of close friends who meet together, visit with each other and do things for each other.

INSTRUMENTATION

Many of the questions used in the construction of the present study's interview schedule were adapted from a questionnaire developed for the study "The Elderly in the Inner City."[2] The questions in that instrument generated data on the activities of daily living for the elderly as well as data on the formal and informal support systems required by the elderly.

However, much of the detailed information generated by the questions provided too fine a measure of the variable of interest, given the small size of the sample. Thus, data analyses focused on selected questions and, in some instances, variables used in the analyses were a consolidation of responses to several questions. Questions applicable only to a very few subjects were eliminated; these will be identified as the variables are described.

DESCRIPTION OF INDEPENDENT VARIABLES

Independent variables used in the data analysis included: (1) five demographic variables; (2) number of living children and three measures of interaction with children; (3) number of siblings living in the metropolitan area; (4) number of relatives living in the metropolitan area; (5) five measures of mobility; (6) three social services measures; and (7) four measures of formal non-senior social group participation.

Demographic variables included: (1) age; (2) family status; (3) sex; (4) ethnicity; and (5) education. The age groups were collapsed into two categories: (1) 60 to 70 years; and (2) 71 years and over. Family status was based on marital status (married or not) and on a count of (natural, adopted or "raised") living children (Question 19, Appendix A). The family status variable itself was organized into three categories:

(1) single/separated/divorced/widowed with no living children;
(2) single/separated/divorced/widowed with living children; and
(3) married with/without living children.

For the ethnicity variable, more than two-thirds of the sample interviewed were Jewish and the numbers in the different ethnic and racial groups were too small to examine separately. Therefore, ethnic groups were dichotomized into Jewish and non-Jewish. Education was grouped as less than a high school diploma, completed high school, or more.

Family Related Variables

Questions 18 and 19 yielded four variables: (1) number of living children; (2) number of children living in the metropolitan New York area; (3) number of children seen at least once a month; and (4) number of children with telephone contact at least weekly.

Number of siblings living in the metropolitan New York City area was derived from Question 27. (See Appendix A for the complete interview.)

Number of relatives living in the metropolitan New York City area was the sum of number of children living in the metropolitan area, plus number of siblings living in the metropolitan area, plus spouse, if married.

Mobility Measures

Question 9 solicited information about distance and modes of transportation to the twelve places visited in the Daily Life Activities (DLA) described in the dependent variables. The five following variables represented the number of places the subjects: (1) traveled ten blocks or less to visit; (2) traveled more than ten blocks to visit; (3) traveled on foot; (4) traveled by public transportation, and (5) traveled by private transportation.

Social Service Agency's Measures

Three questions were included in this measure. Question 14-- "During the past year, have you been to a social service agency?"-- yielded one dichotomous variable.

Question 16 related to "a count of the number of situations in which subjects perceived the formal agency personnel (police, real estate management, church, paid services, etc.) as the major helping source" (see perception of helping sources, page 56).

Question 17 asked the number of social agencies the subject turned to for help during the past year including: (1) Social Security office; (2) the Office for the Aging; (3) Department of Social Services; (4) police; (5) New York City Housing Authority (public housing); (6) senior center; (7) settlement house; (8) visiting nurses' services; (10) family service agency; (11) employment agency; (12) nursing home or home for the aged; (13) minister, priest, rabbi; (14) spiritualist; and (15) other agencies.

Formal Non-Senior Social Group Particiption

Four variables served as indicators for this type of participation-- derived from subitems 3 and 6 of Question 32(c) (frequency of visits to groups or organizations): (1) 32(c)(3), a church or synagogue group (religious organizations); (2) 32(c)(6), other organizations--items 2 (labor unions) and 5 (family circle or club made up of people from your hometown) were eliminated because fewer than 5 respondents belonged to these groups. Item 4 (a senior center or golden age club) was eliminated because everyone visited and the item did not discriminate. Subitem 1 was treated as a dependent variable because it related to self-help groups.

Subject responses were collapsed into two categories for each item: don't visit the group and went to the group rarely to frequently. A third variable, number of groups visited, was created representing a count of the number of non-senior social groups (in Question 32(c)) visited.

A fourth variable derived from Question 32(e) was visited similar groups during earlier life. Subject responses were collapsed into two categories: didn't visit similar groups, and visited groups frequently, occasionally, or rarely.

DESCRIPTION OF DEPENDENT VARIABLES

Daily Life Activities

Questions 9 and 10 on the questionnaire were consolidated to measure the respondents' need for assistance with transportation to the twelve places normally visited in the individual's Daily Life Activities

(DLA) and social life: (1) grocery store; (2) butcher; (3) drugstore; (4) doctor/clinic; (5) clothing store; (6) church/synagogue; (7) bank; (8) park; (9) movie/theater; (10) club/organization; (11) job/business; and (12) bar/restaurant. Four possible responses were provided: (1) *did not go* to the DLA; (2) *went alone* to the DLA; (3) *went with family* to the DLA; or (4) *went with friends* (including neighbors and other group members). A scale also was developed to determine with whom the subjects traveled to the 12 places, the distance traveled, and the mode of transportation (see Appendix F).

The Help Received from Friends Scale

This was a Likert-type scale derived from items in Question 12: "Would you say that members of the groups you belong to do the following things for each other?:

(1) visit with each other;
(2) help you when you are ill;
(5) shop or run errands for you;
(8) provide conversation;
(10) help prepare meals for you, but not keep house;
(11) go on trips together; or
(13) provide moral support in time of crisis.

The response categories for the scale items were recoded to: (1) not at all; (2) only occasionally; (3) fairly often; and (4) very often. Of the original 13 items in Question 12, seven had acceptable item-total correlations and yielded a reliability (internal consistency) coefficient of .74 (Cronbach's Alpha) (see Appendix G). This score was obtained by adding the responses and dividing the answer by the number of items. Contrastingly, the items dropped from this scale for poor item-total correlation (.00 to -.22) were:

(3) give you advice on money matters;
(4) help you make a decision on a big purchase;
(6) give you gifts;
(7) help fix things around the house;
(9) help with minor household tasks; and
(12) help you out with money.

Three of the above items (3, 4 and 6) were analyzed individually; none of the participants indicated that they had participated in any of the latter three activities. Therefore, they were dropped from further analysis. However, one of the items dropped--(7)--was included in the "help received from children scale" and yielded acceptable item-total correlations. In fact, the respondents depended on themselves to accomplish the last two items.

In regard to the poor correlation existing between the six items dropped from the scale and the seven items retained in the scale, the following interpretation is suggested: the items left in the scale appear to measure affective assistance while the six items dropped from the scale measure assistance that was more instrumental in nature. The fact that the two categories were measuring two distinct domains could have accounted for the lack of correlation.

The Help Received from Children Scale

This was a Likert-type scale derived from items in Question 21: "Do your child/children ever help you in any of the following ways?"

(1) help you when you are ill (or when your spouse is ill);
(2) give you advice on money matters;
(3) help you make a decision on a big purchase;
(4) shop or run errands for you;
(5) give you gifts;
(6) help fix things around your house;
(7) keep house for you;
(8) prepare meals for you, but not keep house;
(9) take you away during the summer; or
(11) drive you places such as the doctor, shopping, church, etc.

The answer categories for the scale items were recoded to: (1) not at all; (2) only occasionally; (3) fairly often; and (4) very often. Of the original 11 items in Question 21, 10 had acceptable item-total correlations and yielded a reliability (internal consistency) coefficient of .84 (Cronbach's Alpha) (see Appendix H). This score was obtained by adding the responses and dividing the answer by the number of items. The item dropped from the scale because of an external poor item-total correlation of -.02 was: (10) do your children ever help you out with money? This item was analyzed as an individual dependent variable.

The Help Given to Children Scale

Here again was a Likert-type scale derived from items in Question 20: "Do you ever help your child/children in any of the following ways?"

(1) help out when someone is ill;
(2) shop or run errands;
(5) give gifts;
(6) help your child/children out with money;
(7) fix things around their/his/her house;
(8) give advice on jobs and business mattes;
(9) help them/him/her make a decision on a big purchase, such as car; and
(10) keep house for them/him/her?

The answer categories for the scale items were recoded to: (1) not at all; (2) only occasionally; (3) fairly often; and (4) very often. Of the original 10 items in Question 20, eight had acceptable item-total correlations and yielded a reliability (internal consistency) coefficient of .64 (Cronbach's Alpha) (see Appendix H). This score was obtained by adding the response and dividing the answer by the number of items. The items dropped from the scale because of poor item-total correlations (.01 and -.16) were: (2) babysit for a while when parents are out; and (3) give advice on running a home and bringing up your grandchildren. These items were analyzed as individual dependent variables.

Perception of Helping Sources

These variables were derived from Questions 16, which listed situations where the subjects perceived various others as a major source of help. The three variables represented: (1) the number of situations in which subjects perceived self as the major helping source; (2) the number of situations in which subjects perceived relatives as the major helping source including children and other relatives; and (3) the number of situations in which subjects perceived friends as the major helping source (including friends, neighbors and social activity groups).

The ten situations were: (1) you suddenly feel sick or dizzy; (2) you want to talk to someone about a problem concerning your child or someone else in your family; (3) you need to borrow a few dollars until your next check comes; (4) you feel lonely and want to talk; (5) you need a new light bulb in the ceiling; (6) you need someone to help you get to the doctor; (7) you find you do not have enough money to cover a very big medical bill; (8) you are in the hospital and need someone to look after your apartment; (9) you need someone to help you fill out a form; and (10) you have an accident and need someone to come in each day to bathe and help you take your medicine.

The number of above situations where subjects turned to formal agency personnel (i.e., police, real estate management, church, paid service, etc.) was treated as an independent variable (see Social Service Agencies measures, page 57).

Visits a Group of Friends

Only one subitem from Question 32(c) dealt with informal groups rather than formal organizations; this was 32(c), 1: "a group of close friends who meet together, visit with each other and do things for each other."

Subjects' responses were collapsed into two categories for each item: didn't visit the group and went to the group rarely to frequently.

DATA COLLECTION APPROACH

The researcher designed the interview to obtain data about the variables listed above. Several independent researchers were asked to review the instrument to determine whether the questions measured the correct variables (see Appendix A). An interview pretest was undertaken with eight senior citizens from a social activity center in Manhattan where the activities and demographic characteristics (except for the ethnic makeup in Center 1) were approximately parallel to those in the two centers where the study was conducted. The pretest indicated a need for the material covered in Question 38, which records the activities that the subjects participated in at their respective centers.

During the period of refining the questionnaire, the investigator contacted the general program director of the Associated YM/YWHAs (Associated Ys) to discuss the approach for proceeding with the interviews. At a meeting, it was agreed that he would send the directors of the two Centers a memorandum emphasizing the agency's commitment to the study (see Appendix B) encouraging their support. Each center director was subsequently contacted over the telephone by the researcher and a date was agreed upon for a meeting to discuss the interviews.

As a result of these meetings, it was determined that the data could best be collected face-to-face because the interviews were long and the sample population elderly. The methodology would also allow on-the-spot observation of the ongoing operation of the center's activities and the magnitude of the members' participation. The researcher did all of the interviewing in Center 2 and slightly less than 20 percent of the interviewing in Center 1. Two member volunteers from Center 1 assisted with the interviews at that center. The methodology here could have biased the data received. (This bias was discussed earlier in the section on study sample, page 34).

This procedure in fact was suggested by the center's director and approved by the agency membership officers who believed that this was the best approach since they believed that greater cooperation would be forthcoming if members were involved in conducting the interviews. Two days of training with use of the interview schedule and role-playing was undertaken to assist the two member volunteers with understanding the confidentiality involved in interviewing other residents, developing skill in timing the interviews, keeping it focused and recording exactly what was being said rather than interpreting the answers given. The procedure for obtaining consent from the subjects was reviewed during these sessions (see Appendix C).

For Center 2, where the researcher conducted all of the interviews, the members were informed by the center's director that the survey would be conducted in order to get their own views about the activities of the center and that, hopefully, the information received would help in planning future programs. In addition, some questions would be asked about the ways in which they helped and received help from their families, friends, and neighbors. In Center 1, a letter was sent to the subjects selected from among the registration cards inviting them to a meeting to discuss the survey (see Appendix D). The subjects, with the exceptions stated previously, agreed to participate in the survey. Most preferred to be interviewed by the member volunteers; however, a small percentage (19 percent) preferred to be interviewed by someone unfamiliar to them. The investigator interviewed these.

Each subject was assigned a code number. Thus, names and other personal information which would identify the subjects are not included in this document. Once the interviews were completed the data were coded and keypunched, then transferred to an IBM tape, and subsequently programmed in accordance with the design for the statistical analysis of this study.

Notes

1. A total of 59 senior citizens were interviewed in the two social activities centers. However, during the processing of the data, it was determined that too much information was missing from 11 of the respondents' interview schedules to include them in the sample.

2. The questionnaire referred to here was developed by Marjorie H. Cantor as principal investigator of the research project, "The Elderly in the Inner City," which was completed for the New York City Office for the Aging. The research was supported by a grant from the Administration on Aging, #AA-4-70-089-02. [Questions taken from the study included: 9(a-f), 10, 11, 12, 16, 17, 18 through 32(e).]

IV
FINDINGS

DATA ANALYSIS

The data examined in the present study were, for the most part, categorical (or nominal) and ordinal in nature. Therefore, non-parametric tests were used to examine relationships between variables. The Mann-Whitney U Test or Kruskal-Wallis analysis of variance was used to examine the relationship of demographic group variables with the 17 self-help variables. The Spearman rank-order correlation coefficient was used to examine relationships between the 17 self-help variables and the 14 independent and four dichotomous independent variables.

THE SELF-HELP SUPPORT NETWORK

Chapter IV describes the information gathered on: (1) the elderly's use of self-help; (2) the people with whom they interacted during their participation in self-help activities; (3) their perception of who provided the most help to them; and (4) the extent to which they turned to social service agencies for help. The findings also encompass the meaning of these activities in terms of the elderly carrying out the activities of daily living, engaging in socialization activities, and the assistance the elderly received during times of illness or crisis.

Patterns of Escort Services

In order to determine the level of participation by the elderly in Daily Life Activities (DLA) with whom they participated, the distance they traveled to participate and the mode of transportation used when participating, the subjects were given a list of twelve places (including, grocery store, butcher, drugstore, doctor/clinic, clothing store, church/synagogue, bank, park, movie/theater, club/organization, job/business and bar/restaurant) (see Appendix F). They were asked whether or not they visited any of these places, with whom they went, the distance traveled and the type of transportation used. Of the 12 places the subjects were presented with and asked whether or not they visited to accomplish their Daily Life Activities, data analysis revealed that 100 percent of the subjects were retired and did not go to a job or business; 79 percent did not go to the park; 44 percent did not attend church or synagogue services; 42 percent did not go to the butcher; and 35 percent did not frequent bars or restaurants.

Mobility. The data on mobility indicated that the bulk of the Daily Life Activities (DLA) in which the older persons participated were outside the neighborhood and public transportation was used to reach them--as will be seen in the following discussion of the mobility measures (see Appendix F). Also DLA to which 50 percent or more of the subjects traveled eleven blocks or more to accomplish were: the clothing store, doctor/clinic/ movie/theater and bar/restaurant, butcher and drugstore. An equal number of subjects went to a bank inside or outside of the neighborhood. There were three DLA to which the majority of the subjects traveled less than 10 blocks to accomplish: clubs/organizations (more than 75 percent; church/synagogue (two thirds); and grocery store (more than half).

Most of the DLA to which the subjects went were outside of the neighborhood[1] (11 blocks or more). Seventy-three percent of the subjects went 11 blocks or more to the clothing store; 72 percent went 11 blocks or more to the doctor/clinic; 58 percent went outside of the neighborhood to a movie/theater; 50 percent to the drugstore and bank, respectively. Except for the clubs or organizations located in the two housing developments where the subjects lived, and the grocery store (in Far Rockaway, the subjects operated a food cooperative), the subjects traveled a distance of 11 blocks or more to the DLA.

Transportation. Public transportation was the basic mode of travel for the majority of the subjects (see Appendix K). They traveled on foot to a mean of 2.98 DLA, via public transportation to a mean of 3.06 DLA, and via private transportation to a mean of 1.67 DLA. The majority of subjects walked to two places: club/organization (66 percent) and grocery store (56 percent). A relatively large number walked to church or synagogue (42 percent) or bank (40 percent), followed by the drugstore (35 percent) (see Appendix F). Since the majority of the DLA to which the subjects traveled were located 11 blocks or more away, it was likely that most of the subjects used transportation other than foot to reach them. In fact, the two types of transportation used were public (subway or bus) or private (car owned by the subject's family or friends).

The DLA to which the majority of subjects traveled by public transportation were: movie/theater (46 percent); doctor/clinic (46 percent); clothing store (43 percent); and bank (40 percent). An equal proportion of subjects walked to the bank (see Appendix F). This could have been predicted, since an equal proportion of the subjects banked inside and outside the neighborhood. A relatively large proportion of the subjects, 34 percent, went to bars or restaurants by public transportation. Few of the subjects used private means of travel to the DLA. More specifically, 28 percent went to the doctor/clinic, 20 percent went to the drugstore or the clothing store, and 18 percent went to the grocery store, butcher, and bars/restaurants, respectively, by private transportation. These were likely to be the DLA mostly participated in with family members.

There were 4 places to which at least half of the subjects walked and, with the exception of the drugstore and doctor/clinic, these were the DLA to which at least 50 percent of the subjects traveled alone and also were the DLA located in the neighborhood. These data were not completely consistent with Cantor's result. She found, for example, that the subjects in her study, "are able to and, indeed, do satisfy the bulk of their personal shopping and service needs within the ten-block radius of their self-contained neighborhoods with the exception of medical care."[2] The lack of consistency between Cantor and the findings here could very well relate to the fact that the subjects from the Far Rockaway Center lived in a relatively isolated community at least eleven or more blocks from the DLA. These subjects had to go beyond the neighborhood to satisfy the bulk of their personal needs.

Escort patterns. The 5 Daily Life Activities (DLA) to which the greatest percentage of subjects went alone were: doctor/clinic (65 percent); bank (56 percent); drugstore (54 percent); grocery store (48 percent); and club or organization (44 percent) (see Appendix F). A range of from 13 percent to 25 percent of the subjects went with family to 9 DLA. Those activities included: clothing store (25 percent); grocery store (23 percent); doctor/clinic (21 percent); church/synagogue, bank, movie/theater (each 17 percent); butcher and drugstore (15 percent); and bar/restaurants (13 percent). A range of 10 percent to 27 percent of the subjects went with friends to eight of the DLA. These activities included: bar/restaurants (27 percent), movie/theater and clothing store (21 percent), bank (17 percent), grocery store (15 percent), drugstore and club/organizations (13 percent), and butcher (10 percent).

The DLA to which the lowest percentage of subjects went with friends were church/synagogue, doctor/clinic, and the park. The DLA to which the larger percentage of subjects went with neighbors were very negligible except for the grocery store (8 percent) or the butcher (8 percent). Only 3 of the DLA were visited with group members of the social activities groups: 21 percent of the subjects went with group members to the movie/theater, 17 percent to club/organizations and 15 percent to bar/restaurants (see Appendix F).

More than 50 percent of the subjects either went to 10 of the 12 DLA alone or did not go to them at all. The 2 DLA to which more than 50 percent of the subjects went with others were of the socialization or leisure-time-type activities movie/theater (61 percent) and bar/restaurants (57 percent). These 2 places were visited with friends, family and group members.

When the relationship between the mobility variables and the patterns of escort variables were looked at, the data indicated that the mobility variables were more strongly related to the friends' variables. The DLA to which the majority of subjects traveled out of the neighborhood (except for doctor/clinic) were of the socialization type (i.e., clothes shopping, movie/theater, and bar/restaurant). Except for clothes shopping, these activities were the activities to which the subjects more frequently chose friends to accompany them. The data indicated that subjects who traveled more than 10 blocks to the DLA did so mostly with friends while those who went alone to these activities did so within the neighborhood. Places traveled to via public transportation was also strongly to moderately correlated with visits a group of friends, go to DLA with friends, and help received from friends.

Help Received from Friends

The literature basically supports the position that the family, both immediate and extended, is the main source of support for the elderly. However, many researchers including Litwak et al., Cantor, and Wentowski provide empirical evidence of the use of friends and neighbors to help maintain the elderly in the community.[3] In this study, the subjects were asked whether they used their friends (included in the scale where neighbors and group members of the social activity centers) to help out with Daily Life Activities (DLA) and to provide emotional and social support under various circumstances (see Appendix G). The sample mean for the 7 help-from-friends scale items was 1.88 (scale range: 1 = not at all, through 3 = fairly often). The greatest help from friends was: "provide conversation" ($\bar{x} = 3.0$); followed by "visit with each other" ($\bar{x} = 2.3$); "go on trips together" ($\bar{x} = 2.1$); "help you when you are ill" ($\bar{x} = 1.7$). The least help from friends was "help prepare meals" ($\bar{x} = 1.0$).

The help-from-friends scale indicated that the subjects could and did rely on their friends for help, on the average, for about 2 out of the 7 items in the scale. These items were basically in the area of visiting with and providing conversation for them followed by going on trips together. Apparently, these were trips to the theater/movie or to restaurants, and provided socialization types of activities.

The six items dropped from the scale for poor item-total correlations add little increase to the level of help from friends when examined as independent items. One item, "give you gifts" ($\bar{x} = 1.4$), indicated a minimum level of help from friends.

Both Mayer and Cantor reported socialization as a major factors in elderly-neighborhood relationships. Cantor went so far as to say that, "the importance of the neighborhood as a socialization center for older people cannot be underestimated."[4] This socialization process, with the help of the staff of the two centers, extended beyond the borders of the neighborhood during the trips to the theater/movies, restaurants and shopping. Indeed, the staff of the two social activities centers indicated that the center frequently planned group trips to theater/movies and restaurants, accounting perhaps, for a large percentage of attendance with others at these activities.

Family Related Activities and Self-Help

Many writers who are supporters of self-help activities for the elderly have suggested that family members can no longer be expected to provide the major portion of care for their families. Some reasons given for this are that family members of the elderly may be elderly themselves; the social and economic costs for this help is too great; and that they live at great distance from the elderly.[5] Lopata reported "interaction with friends, neighbors, siblings, children, and other kin are at best sporadic throughout the period of widowhood."[6] However, other supporters of self-help for the elderly maintained that family have always interacted and provided varying types of support for their elderly kin. Among these are Wentowski, Mayer, Cantor, and Abrahams. They also suggested that the exchange was mutual between the elderly and their children, as the present data have indicated.[7]

The subjects had an average of 1.5 living children. This figure broke down into less than one child per subject living in the metropolitan area ($\bar{x} = 0.65$), less than one child per subject who was seen monthly or more ($\bar{x} = 0.70$), and an average of slightly more than one child per subject ($\bar{x} = 1.21$) who telephoned at least weekly. Each subject had an average of less than one sibling living in the metropolitan area ($\bar{x} = 0.69$) and an average of 1.5 relatives residing in the metropolitan area. Thus, all of the subjects had an average of one nearby relative or within the metropolitan New York City area; all of the subjects had an average of one child who contacted the subject by telephone at least weekly (see Appendix K).

Help received from children. The sample mean for the 10 help-received-from children scale items was 1.37 (scale range: 1 = not at all, through 4 = very often)[8] (see Appendix H). The greatest help received from children was receipt of gifts ($\bar{x} = 2.0$) followed by "help you when you are ill, or when your spouse is ill" ($\bar{x} = 1.8$), "shop or run errands for you" ($\bar{x} = 1.6$), and "drive you places such as the doctor, shopping, etc." ($\bar{x} = 1.5$). The least help from children was "keep house for you" ($\bar{x} = 1.0$). The one item dropped from the original scale for poor item-total correlations, when examined independently, also indicated that the subjects received no help from children in the financial area. The mean score for "help you out with money" was ($\bar{x} = 1.0$).

Help given to children by the elderly. The sample mean for the eight help-given-to-children scale items was 1.30 (scale range: 1 = not at all, through 4 = very often) (see Appendix I). The greatest help given to children by the elderly was "give gifts" ($\bar{x} = 2.2$), followed by "help out when someone is ill" ($\bar{x} = 1.5$), and "help your child/children out with money" ($\bar{x} = 1.3$). The subjects never gave help to children in the following areas: "fix things around their/his/her house" ($xx = 1.0$), "help them/him/her make a decision on a big purchase, such as a car" ($\bar{x} = 1.0$), and "keep house for them/him/her" ($\bar{x} = 1.0$).

The two items dropped from the original scale for poor item-total correlations, when examined individually, indicated that the subjects did not "babysit with their grandchildren ($\bar{x} = 1.0$) or "give their children advice on running the home and bringing up the grandchildren" ($\bar{x} = 1.0$). Given the ages of the subjects, the explanation here could be that the grandchildren were beyond the age for babysitting or advice about bringing them up.

Apparently, giving gifts was the highest level of exchange between the subjects and their children with the frequency of subjects giving gifts to their children slightly greater ($\bar{x} = 2.2$) compared to gifts received from children ($\bar{x} = 2.0$). The next highest level of exchange was helping out when someone was ill. Here, the children provided a slightly higher level of help. The mean for giving help to children was ($\bar{x} = 1.5$) and the mean for receiving help from children was ($xx = 1.8$). Because failing health tends to increase with age, it would be logical to assume that the subjects were ill more frequently than their children, thus requiring more assistance during illness. However, the present study's data did not support this assumption.[9]

The study indicated that the majority of the subjects had at least one child who contacted them weekly, showing a clear pattern of interaction between subjects and children (if they had children) and an indication that subjects dependent on children for help and were willing to give help to children. Gift-giving was the highest level of exchange here. It occurred both ways with slightly more older people giving gifts than they received from their children. The second level of exchange between subjects and their children was in the area of illness or health emergencies. The children assisted slightly more in this area. These results were consistent with findings reported separately by Mayer and Cantor who both analyzed data from the "Inner City Elderly Study."[10]

This was also true for Wentowski's research where she found that "A majority of the people in this study did actually rely heavily on one or more close kinspersons. Seventy percent of them have one or more children with whom they have significant exchanges."[11]

Perception of Helping Sources

In order to collect data on whom the subjects perceived as being most willing to provide help, a list of 10 situations where they might need help was presented to them.[12] They were also given four alternative sources of help from which to choose: self, relatives (including children and other relatives), friends (including friends, neighbors, and members of the social activities groups), and social services agencies.[13]

In various social, economic or health-related situations requiring assistance, the subjects relied on friends ($\bar{x}$ = 2.98) followed by reliance on relatives ($\bar{x}$ = 2.65), then on social service agencies ($\bar{x}$ = 2.25) and, finally, on their own skills ($\bar{x}$ = 2.12) (see Appendix L). The subjects filled out their own forms, for instance, but asked friends or neighbors for help if they became suddenly dizzy, sick or needed to discuss a problem about a child or other family member. For help with emergency cash, or routine help with getting to the doctor, they called a relative. Finally, they turned to a social service agency for extended or consistent medical care.

The perception-of-helping-sources data indicated that the subjects depended on themselves, their relatives, and friends with almost equal frequency. However, a clear distinction existed among the nature of things for which they turned to different sources. For example, the subjects filled out forms for themselves most of the time; if they needed assistance in this area they turned to a social service agency. They looked to a friend or neighbor in an emergency requiring immediate attention such as "sudden illness or dizziness." However, for help with money, or help with routinely getting to the doctor, they sought help from relatives.

These perceptions are supported by Litwak et al. in their study of older people in New York and Florida which suggested that "a primary group can optimally handle tasks which match it in structure."[14]

Litwak, et al. developed a "differential primary group structure on types of tasks exchanged."[15] The researchers provided data from a survey of 1,746 people, 65 years of age or older, located in the New York City metropolitan area and in Dade and Broward Counties in Florida. These data suggested activities that most appropriately matched each primary group structure, e.g., neighbors were chosen to watch the subjects' house when they were out shopping, or as the person from whom to borrow small household items when the subjects needed something in a hurry. Friends were chosen for favorite free-time activities. However, activities that suggested long-term commitment, but did not require continuous close proximity, such as checking up on the person on a regular basis or talking to him or her on the telephone about personal problems, were considered as something appropriate for a relative to do.

USE OF FORMAL AGENCIES

Use of Social Service Agencies

Several questions gathered information about the elderly's use of assistance other than the self-help networks. The subjects were asked whether or not they had turned to a social service agency during the past year. They were given a list of 15 agencies to indicate which ones they had used (see Appendix J). Only 22 percent had turned to social services agencies (see Table 2). Those subjects turned to an average of 1.22 social agencies for help with difficulties experienced during the past year (see Appendix K). The two social agencies turned to by most of the subjects were senior centers (33 percent) and social security office (27 percent) (see Appendix J).

Various writers have discussed the desire for independence by the elderly, perhaps accounting for their not seeking help from any source, but especially from social services agencies until probably no other alternative existed. Cantor and Mayer stated:

> The elderly in the inner city neighborhood, like all older people, are fiercely independent and their responses to a series of hypothetical situations pertaining to services needs and sources of assistance indicated that, in most cases, their initial reaction is to try to manage on their own, or if necessary turn

to the members of the informal support system with whom they have a primary relationship, such as a child, intimate or neighbor. Community agencies are referred to primarily when personal or family resources are exhausted, non-existent or when the type of assistance required is beyond the capacity of the informal support system.[16]

Table 2
Frequencies for Use of Social Service Agencies During the Past Year (N=48)

| | Used a Social Service Agency During Past Year | |
	N	Percent
Yes	10	22.0
No	36	78.0
Missing data	2	--
Total	48	100.0

This study also attempted to ascertain the subjects' perceptions of major helping sources. The alternatives suggested were self, relatives, friends (discussed earlier in the chapter), and social service agencies. The social service agencies ($\bar{x}$ = 2.25) were chosen only slightly more frequently than the alternative self ($\bar{x}$ = 2.12) (see Appendices K and L). The types of help for which the subjects turned to the formal agencies were help with replacing a light bulb in the ceiling (54 percent), and in case of an accident which required help on a daily basis with bathing and taking medicine (52 percent). A lower percentage sought help from the social service agencies with "money to pay a big medical bill" (33 percent); "help you get to the doctor" (29 percent); and "help on filling out forms" (23 percent) (see Appendix J).

Use of Formal Non-Senior Citizens' Social Group Participation

The present study addressed to what extent the subjects participated in other formal social groups which were not specifically for the elderly (i.e., religious organizations, YW/YMHA, hiking clubs, fraternal organizations, Hadassah Women, political clubs, workmen benefits fund, and charitable organizations). The sample mean for number of formal non-senior groups visited was 1.96 (*sd*=0.97), with a median of 1.8 and a range of 1 to 4 (see Appendix K).

Table 3 presents frequencies for the three formal non-senior social group variables: (1) visits to religious organizations; (2) visits to other organizations; and (3) earlier life activities (that is, visited similar groups in earlier life).

Table 3
Frequencies for Use of Formal Non-Senior Social Group Participation:
Religious Organizations, Other Organizations, and Similar Groups in
Earlier Life (N=48)

	N	*Percent*
Visit a religious organization		
rarely to frequently		
Yes	14	29.0
No	34	71.0
Total	48	100.0
Visit other organizations		
rarely to farequently		
Yes	13	27.0
No	35	73.0
Total	48	100.0
Members of similar groups		
in earlier life		
Yes	23	48.0
No	25	52.0
Total	48	100.0

Except for visits to similar groups in earlier life (48 percent reported visits to similar non-senior social groups during their earlier life), less than a third of the subjects reported involvement in the above agencies or organizations. Twenty-nine percent visited religious organizations and 27 percent visited "other organizations." Frequencies for use of formal non-senior social group participation: religious organizations other organizations and similar groups in earlier life.

THE RELATIONSHIP OF DEMOGRAPHIC CHARACTERISTICS OF THE ELDERLY TO PATTERNS OF SELF-HELP ACTIVITIES

The demographic variables were examined with the seventeen self-help variables to determine whether the demographic variables impacted significantly on the level of self-help activities in which the subjects engaged. Tables 4 through 8 summarize the differences found when the demographic variables were examined.

Age

The findings showed that older members of the groups studied gave to and received more help from their children than younger subjects. The older subjects gave and received help at about the same level of frequency (see Table 4). Using discrete scores on help received from children, a Mann-Whitney U Test revealed that the mean rank for subjects 71 years of age and over, 27.5, was significantly higher than the mean rank for subjects 60 to 70 years of age, 18.9 ($U = 169.5$, $z = 2.12$, $p < .05$). On the help-given-to-children scale, a Mann-Whitney U Test revealed that the mean rank for subjects 71 years and over, 27.0, was significantly higher than the mean rank for subjects 60 to 70 years of age, 18.5 ($U = 161.0$, $z = 2.17$, $p < .05$).

The analysis of the age variable indicated, as stated above, that older subjects gave and received more than younger subjects. It seems safe to suggest that the younger subjects might still have been married and dependent on their spouses for the greater portion of the exchange. This hypothesis is supported by Lopata and The New York State Office on Aging's "Caregivers Report." Lopata found that widows in urban communities which she studied indicated that the most supportive relationship for the elderly was with the living spouse. The State Office on Aging's study also reported the spouse as the most supportive relationship and as the greatest source of help.[17] The present study suggests that where there was a nuclear family, they tended to depend on each other for the greatest exchange. As will be seen in the following discussion of Table 5, the exchanges between the unmarried subjects and their children were greater than between the married subjects and their children.

Table 4

Relationships Between Age and Help Received from and Help Given to Children (N=48)

	Mann-Whitney U Test		
	Mean Rank	N	U (z)
Help Received from Children Scale			169.5
			2.12*
60-70	18.9	19	
71 years and over	27.5	29	
Help Given to Children Scale			161.0
			2.17*
60-70 years	18.5	19	
71 years and over	27.0	29	

*p < .05

Table 5
Relationships Between Family Status and Go Alone to the Daily Life
Activities: Help Received from Children Scale and Help Given to
Children Scale (N=48)

	Kruskal-Wallis One-Way ANOVA		
	Mean Rank	N	Chi Square
Go alone			5.9*
Family Status			
Not married/no children	33.9	9	
Not married/children	21.8	29	
Married	21.0	9	
Total		47[a]	
Help Received from Children Scale			23.0**
Family status			
Not married/no children	8.0	9	
Not married/children	31.1	29	
Married	17.2	9	
Total		47[a]	
Help Given to Children Scale			22.4**
Family Status			
Not married/no children	7.0	9	
Not married/children	30.2	29	
Married	19.2	9	
Total		47[a]	

[a]One subject missing on Family Status

*p < .05   *p < .001

Family status. These groups differed significantly on three self-help variables: go alone to the Daily Life Activities (DLA), help received from children and help given to children (see Table 5). Using discrete scores on "go alone," a Kruskal-Wallis one-way analysis of variance revealed that the mean rank for subjects who were not married and had no children, 33.9 was significantly higher than the mean rank for subjects who were not married but had children, 21.8, and for married subjects, 21.0 ($X^2 = 5.9$, p < .05).

The data indicated that the subjects who had neither spouse nor children tended to go alone to the DLA much more frequently than either the subjects who were not married but had children or the married subjects. The subjects who were not married but had children and the married subjects tended to go alone to the DLA at about the same level of frequency. One might surmise that the subjects who went alone more frequently might have established a pattern of going alone during earlier years. This hypothesis is supported by Sherman who suggested that perhaps older persons without children have, by necessity, developed lifelong habits of independence.[18]

On help received from children, the Kruskal-Wallis one-way analysis of variance revealed that the mean rank for subjects who were not married but had children, 31.1, was significantly higher than the mean rank for married subjects, 17.2, ($X^2 = 23.0$, p < .001). For this variable, the subjects with no spouse but children received help from children almost twice as frequently as the married subjects.

On help given to children, the Kruskal-Wallis one-way analysis of variance revealed that the mean rank for subjects who were not married but had children, 30.2, was significantly higher than the mean rank for married subjects, 19.2, ($X^2 = 22.4$, p < .001). As with the help received from children, the subjects who had children but no spouse gave a great deal more to their children than the married subjects. The exchange between the two is about even with the subjects receiving slightly more from the children. Since the statistics for the age variable indicated that older subjects gave and received more than the younger subjects, the more plausible explanation is that the married subjects were younger and possibly still depended on their spouses for the greater portion of the exchange. Furthermore, one could hypothesize that because the older subjects depended on their children more, they felt the need to reciprocate. This view is supported by Wentowski's discussion on reciprocity where she indicated that "the most basic cultural rule governing reciprocity is that something received requires something returned."[19]

Sex

This variable accounted for significant difference on two dependent variables: (1) go with friends to Daily Life Activities (DLA); and (2) friends help you make a decision on a big purchase (an unscaled item on help received from friends) (Table 6). Using discrete scores on "go with friends," a Mann-Whitney U Test revealed that the mean rank for males, 11.6, was significantly lower than the mean rank for females, 26.0 (U=43.0, z=2.22, p<.05). The analysis indicated that the male subjects were less like to go to daily life activities with their friends than the female subjects; however, the male subjects were more likely to request their friends' advice when making a big purchase. When the males were asked who they were likely to request advice from regarding a decision on a big purchase item, the Mann-Whitney U Test revealed that the mean rank for males, 33.1, was significantly higher than the mean rank for females, 23.5 (U=64.5, z=4.19, p<.001).

Ethnicity

Ethnic groups differed significantly on two variables: (1) Subjects go alone to the DLA; and (2) help subjects received from friends (see Table 7). Using discrete scores on "Subjects go alone," a Mann-Whitney U Test revealed that the mean rank for Jewish subjects, 21.8, was significantly lower than the mean rank for non-Jewish subjects, 31.7 (U=134.0, z=2.20, p<.05). On help from friends, a Mann-Whitney U Test revealed that the mean rank for Jewish subjects 27.2, was significantly higher than the mean rank for non-Jewish subjects, 17.1, (U=131.5, z=2.24, p<.05).

Thus, the data revealed that the non-Jewish subjects tended to go alone to the DLA more frequently than the Jewish subjects. Two reasons could have accounted for this: First, the non-Jewish subjects lived in an area where performance of the DLA was more feasible than in Far Rockaway where more of the Jewish subjects lived; second, because the Jewish subjects traveled more frequently out of the neighborhood to perform most of their DLA, and because staff of the

Table 6

Relationship Between Sex and Go with Friends to the Daily Life Activities and Friends Help You Make a Decision on a Big Purchase (N=48)

	Mann-Whitney U Test[a]		
	Mean Rank	N	U (z)
Go with friends			43.0 (2.22)*
Male	11.6	5	
Female	26.0	43	
Help you make a decision on a big purchase			64.5 (4.19)**
Male	33.1	5	
Female	23.5	43	

[a]To obtain the ranking in Tables 6, 7, and 8, the groups were combined and the cases were ranked in order of increasing size (i.e., in ranking from 1 to 10, 1=least activity/interaction and 10-greatest activity/interaction).

*p < .05   **p < .001

Table 7
*Relationships Between Ethnicity and Go Alone to the Daily Life
Activities and Help Received from Friends Scale*

	Mean Rank	N	U (z)
	Mann-Whitney U Test[a]		
Go alone			134.0 (2.20)*
Jewish	21.8	35	
Non-Jewish	31.7	13	
Help Received from Friends Scale			131.5 (2.24)*
Jewish	27.2	35	
Non-Jewish	17.1	13	

[a]To obtain the ranking in Tables 6, 7, and 8, the groups were
combined and the cases were ranked in order of increasing size (i.e.,
in ranking from 1 to 10, 1=least activity/interaction and 10-greatest
activity/interaction).

*p < .05

senior center to which they belonged planned many group trips for them, they traveled to most of the activities with someone.[20] The help-received-from-friends scale also revealed that the Jewish subjects received help from their friends more frequently than the non-Jewish subjects. One of the above explanations could also have accounted for this fact.

In summary, that the majority of Jewish subjects lived in an isolated homogeneous community might have encouraged them to rely more on friends as well as to interact more with their friends. Another reason could have been that the children of the Jewish subjects lived farther away than those of the non-Jewish subjects and, according to many of the subjects, they were preoccupied with their own families and businesses, making it difficult for them to spend much time with the subjects. Since the friends lived closer and were more readily available, the subjects turned to them.

Education

The education variable differed significantly in its relationships to three dependent variables: (1) number of Daily Life Activities (DLA) gone to with family; (2) help-given-to-children scale; and (3) number of situations when friends were perceived as the major helping source (see Table 8). Using discrete scores on go with family, a Mann-Whitney U Test revealed that the mean rank was significantly greater for subjects with at least a high school education, 28.6, compared to subjects with an education of 11 years or less, 20.1 ($U = 186.0$, $z = 2.37$, $p < .05$). The data revealed that the more educated subjects tended to go places with their family more frequently than the less educated. This also applied to the help-given-to-children scale in that the more educated subjects gave more help to their children than the less educated.

On the help-given-to-children scale, a Mann-Whitney U Test revealed that the mean rank for subjects with at least a high school education, 28.6, was significantly greater than for subjects with an education of 11 years or less, 19.7 ($U = 179.5$, $z = 2.08$, $p < .05$). On the other hand, the data also showed that the less educated subjects perceived their friends as the people to whom they would turn when needing help. A Mann-Whitney U Test revealed that subjects with 11

Table 8
Relationships Between Education and Go with Family to the Daily Life
Activities: Help Given to Children Scale and Subjects' Perception of
Friends as the Major Helping Source (N=48)

Number of Daily Life Activities	Mann-Whitney U Test[a]		
	Mean Rank	N	U (z)
Go with family			186.0 (2.37)*
11 years or less	20.1	23	
High school or more	28.6	25	
Help Given to Children Scale			179.5 (2.08)*
11 years or less	19.7	23	
High school or more	28.6	25	
Subjects' perceptions of friends as the major helping source			183.0 (2.18)*
11 years or less	29.0	23	
High school or more	20.3	25	

[a]To obtain the ranking in Tables 6, 7, and 8, the groups were combined and the cases were ranked in order of increasing size (i.e., in ranking from 1 to 10, 1=least activity/interaction and 10=greatest activity/intraction).

*p<.05

years of education or less (mean rank = 29.0) named their friends as the major helping source more frequently than subjects with at least a high school education (mean rank = 20.3) (U=183.0, z=2.18, p<.05).

In summary, the elderly subjects most likely to participate in self-help activities were the older members of the centers who had no spouse, but who did have living children with whom they interacted. They were, for the most part, female Jewish subjects who had at least a high school diploma.

Self-Help With Family Related Measures

The relationship between self-help measures and six family related measures were examined using Spearman rank-order correlation coefficients (see Table 9). Two of the self-help measures were strongly related to all but one of the family related measures (number of siblings in the metropolitan area). The help-received-from-children scale had strong positive correlations with number of living children (r=.67, p<.001) and number of children who telephoned weekly (r=.68, p<.001). This scale also had moderately strong positive correlations with the number of children in the metropolitan area (r=.45, p<.001) and the number of children seen monthly (r=.43, p<.001). In addition, it had positive correlations with number of relatives living in the metropolitan area (r=.33, p<.01). Possibly, the latter relationship was diluted in value because the number of siblings living in the metropolitan area was included to make up this variable and there was no relationship between it and the self-help measures discussed.

The second self-help measure, which had strong correlations with the family related measures, was the help-given-to-children scale, which had strong positive correlations with four of the family related measures: (1) number of living children (r=.70, p<.001); (2) number of children living in the metropolitan area (r=.57, p<.001); (3) number of children with telephone contacts at least weekly (r=.73, p<.001); and (4) number of relatives living in the metropolitan area (r=.47, p<.001). As with the former self-help measure, number of siblings living in the metropolitan area had no significant relationship to the self-help measure and, because it was included in the three variables which made up the relatives measure, it possibly reduced the

Table 9
Spearman Rank Order Correlation Coefficients for Relationships Between Seventeen Self-Help Measures and Six Family-Related Measures (N=48)

	No. of Children Living	No. of Children in Metro Area	No. of Children Seen Monthly	No. of Children with Weekly Phone	No. of Siblings in Metro Area	No. of Relatives in Metro Area
Number of Daily Life Activities						
Don't go	.05	.01	.01	.06	-.17	-.08
Go alone	-.10	.01	-.19	-.23	-.17	-.16
Go with family	.01	.19	.19	.06	.15	.34**
Go with friends	.03	-.15	-.07	-.17	.08	.14
Help Received from Friends Scale	.14	-.01	.12	.05	.24*	.11
Friends give you advice on money matters	.02	.01	-.01	.09	-.01	-.06
Friends help you make a decision on a big purchase	.18	.00	.02	-.15	.00	.04
Friends give you gifts	.27*	.10	.00	.11	-.07	.15
Help Received from Children Scale	.67***	.45***	.43***	.68***	.14	.33**
Children help you out with money	.21	-.11	-.13	-.18	-.12	-.04

Table 9 (continued)

	No. of Children Living	No. of Children in Metro Area	No. of Children Seen Monthly	No. of Children with Weekly Phone	No. of Siblings in Metro Area	No. of Relatives in Metro Area
Help Given to Children Scale	.70***	.57***	.63***	.73***	.17	.47***
Babysit grandchildren	.06	.13	.07	.08	.07	.15
Give advice on running a home and bringing up grandchildren	.16	.26*	-.01	.09	-.18	.16
Subjects' Perception of Major Helping Source						
Turn to self	.19	.28*	.29*	.09	-.06	.18
Turn to relatives	.05	.29*	.29*	.14	.04	.13
Turn to friends	-.20	-.40**	-.39**	-.15	.06	-.15
Visits a Group of Friends	.02	.04	-.05	.08	.27*	.19

*p < .05   **p < .01   ***p < .001

degree to which that measure correlated with the self-help measure. The self-help measure, "go with family," had positive correlations with the number of relatives living in the metropolitan area ($r = .34$, $p < .01$).

The help-received-from-friends scale correlated positively with number of siblings in the metropolitan area ($r = .24$, $p < .05$). Friends give you gifts correlated positively with number of living children ($r = .27$, $p < .05$). Give the children advice on running a home and bringing up grandchildren correlated positively with number of children in the metropolitan area ($r = .26$, $p < .05$).

The comparison of the self-help measures with the family-related measures indicated clear interaction between the subjects and their families if they had relatives. This interaction was strongest between the subjects and their children, for the subjects both depended on their children for help and helped their children. This finding parallels those of a number of researchers including Cantor, Litwak et al., and Wentowski. The finding was also consistent, as will be seen below, with the subjects' perceptions of their greatest helping sources.

Perceptions of Helping Sources and Family Related Measures

The relationship between the subjects' perception of their helping sources and the 6 family-related measures indicated almost equally positive relationships between 4 pairs. The subjects' perception of themselves as the major source of help had positive correlations with two family related measures: the number of children living in the metropolitan area ($r = .28$, $p < .05$) and the number of children seen at least monthly ($r = .29$, $p < .05$). The perception of relatives as the major helping source correlated with two family related measures: the number of children living in the metropolitan area ($r = .29$, $p < .05$) and the number of children seen monthly ($r = 29$, $p. < .05$). The "visits a group of friends" measure correlated with the number of siblings in the metropolitan area ($r = .27$, $p < .05$) (see Table 9). In addition, to the extent that the subjects interacted with family members, they apparently did not perceive their friends as major helping sources. If they did turn to friends, it was for different things as indicated in the discussion on mobility variables later in the chapter. The subjects' perception of their friends as the major source of help had moderately negative correlations with two family related measures: the number of children living in the metropolitan area (r=-.40, p<.01), and the number of children seen at least monthly (r=-.39, p<.01). The data here seem to indicate, then, that if the subjects had children whom they saw at least monthly, they felt they could rely on these children for help and thus did not need their friends for such help.

Self-Help With Mobility

The self-help measures were compared to the 5 mobility measures in order to ascertain whether the location of the Daily Life Activities (DLA), the distance traveled to perform them, and/or the type of transportation used to implement them had impacted on either use of self-help or the subjects' perceptions of who helped them most. The relationship between 17 measures of self-help and 5 measures of mobility were examined using Spearman rank-order correlation coefficients (see Table 10).

Distance traveled. The strongest positive correlation was between number of DLA traveled more than '10 blocks to perform and number of DLA gone to with friends (r=.61, p<.001). The number of DLA traveled more than 10 blocks to perform had a moderately strong correlation with the help-received-from-friends scale (r=.50, p<.001). The number of DLA traveled more than 10 blocks to perform was also correlated with visits a group of friends (r=.30, p<.05). The number of DLA traveled 10 blocks or less to perform correlated with number of DLA gone to alone (r=.33, p<.01) and with friends help you make a decision on a big purchase (r=.27, p<.05). There were moderately strong negative correlations between the number of DLA to which the subjects did not go and the number of DLA traveled more than 10

Table 10

Spearman Rank-Order Correlation Coefficients for Relationships Between Seventeen Self-Help Measures and Five Mobility Measures (N = 48)

	Number of Daily Life Activities				
	10 Blocks or Less	More than 10 Blocks	On Foot	Via Public	Via Private
Number of Daily Life Activities					
Don't go	-.07	-.54***	-.04	-.36**	-.04
Go alone	.33**	-.25*	.30*	.40**	-.20
Go with family	.13	-.04	.00	-.17	.20
Go with friends	-.30*	.61***	-.22	.34**	.09
Help Received from Friends Scale	-.20	.50***	-.16	.33**	.05
Friends give you advice on money matters	-.05	-.15	.00	-.08	-.04
Friends help you make a decision on a big purchase	.27*	-.27*	.11	-.28*	.17
Friends give you gifts	.05	-.05	.13	.02	.06
Help Received from Children Scale	-.30*	.18	-.18	.02	.05
Children help you out with money	.17	-.09	.15	.03	-.13

Table 10 (continued)

	Number of Daily Life Activities				
	10 Blocks or Less	More than 10 Blocks	On Foot	Via Public	Via Private
Help Given to Children Scale	-.13	.07	-.14	-.10	.07
Babysit grandchildren	-.05	-.09	.00	-.09	.08
Give advice on running a home and bringing up grandchildren	.19	-.06	.24*	.01	-.05
Subjects Perceptions of Major Helping Sources					
Turn to self	.01	.14	-.14	-.13	.30*
Turn to relatives	.12	-.10	.21	-.12	.00
Turn to friends	-.05	.00	-.05	.25*	-.25*
Visits a Group of Friends	-.15	.30*	-.08	.47***	-.25*

*p<.05 **p<.01 ***p<.001

blocks to perform ($r=-.54$, $p<.001$). The number of DLA traveled 10 blocks or more to perform also had negative correlations with friends help you make a decision on a big purchase ($r=-.27$, $p<.05$) and the number of DLA traveled to alone ($r=-.25$, $p<.05$). The number of DLA traveled 10 blocks or less to perform had negative correlations with the number of DLA gone with friends ($r=-.30$, $p<.05$) and the help-received-from-children scale ($r=-.30$, $p<.05$).

Based on the data, one might surmise that subjects who traveled more than 10 blocks to the DLA did so mostly with friends, but these same subjects traveled mostly alone to activities inside the neighborhood.

Transportation. The strongest correlations for transportation with self-help variables were between number of DLA traveled to via public transportation and visits with a group of friends ($r=.47$, $p<.001$). The number of DLA traveled to via public transportation correlated with the number of DLA gone to with friends ($r=.34$, $p<.01$) and help received from friends ($r=.33$, $p<.01$). Here, the friends were perceived as a major helping source ($r=.25$, $p<.05$). However, there were negative correlations between the number of DLA traveled to via public transportation, and the number of DLA to which the subjects did not go ($r=-.36$, $p<.01$) and between the number of DLA traveled to via public transportation and friends help you make a decision on a big purchase ($r=-.28$, $p<.05$).

Two self-help measures were correlated with the number of DLA traveled to by foot: (1) number of DLA gone to alone ($R=.30$, $p<.05$); and (2) giving the children advice on running the home and bringing up your grandchildren ($r=.24$, $p<.05$). The number of DLA traveled to via private transportation was correlated with the subjects' perceptions of self as the major helping source ($r=.30$, $p<.05$), which suggests that those subjects who had private transportation (own or family) dependent on themselves more in situations requiring help from others. Number of DLA traveled to via private transportation had negative correlations with the subjects' perceptions of friends as a major source ($r=-.25$, $p<.05$) and visits with a group of friends ($r=-.25$, $p<.05$).

The mobility variables clearly were related more strongly to the friends variables. Earlier in this chapter (page 53) it was pointed out that the DLA to which the subjects traveled more frequently out of the neighborhood were of the socialization type (i.e., shopping, 72 percent, movie/theater 58 percent, and bar/restaurants 50 percent (see Appendix F). Except for shopping, these were the activities to which the subjects more frequently chose friends to accompany them. Thus, the data on the mobility variables appeared to have positive relationships only with those activities involving friends, usually for recreational or socialization purposes. Whether they traveled 10 blocks or less, or 11 blocks or more, to participate in DLA did not appear to affect their relationships with family members or their dependence on them for help under various circumstances. Traveling more than 10 blocks and using public transportation, however, did have some effect on whether they did or did not go to the DLA. In fact, there was a strong negative correlation between the subjects going more than 10 blocks to the DLA and their not going to the DLA at all.

Self-Help and Use of Formal Service Delivery

No strong relationship was found between use or non-use of social service agencies and the self-help variables; however, the slight relationship which did exist indicated that the subjects turned to formal agencies for help when they perceived that self-help or their families' help was unavailable to them. However, it did not affect their interaction with friends.

The relationships between the self-help measures and subjects' use of social service agencies, perceptions of formal agencies as a major helping source, and number of agencies to which subjects turned were examined using Spearman rank-order correlation coefficients (see Table 11). The only self-help measure correlated with the use of social service agencies was the number of Daily Life Activities (DLA) gone to alone ($r = .24$, $p < .05$). The number of situations when the subjects perceived the formal agencies as the major helping source

Table 11

Spearman Rank-Order Correlation Coefficients for Relationships Between Seventeen Self-Help Measures and Perception of Helping Source and Use of Social Service Agency Measures (N=48)

	Use Social Service Agencies[a]	Number Perceived Formal Agencies as Helping Source	Number Agencies to Which Subjects Turned
Number of Daily Life Activities			
Don't go	-.21	.01	.15
Go alone	.24*	.21	-.07
Go with family	-.08	-.29*	.04
Go with friends	.00	.18	-.01
Help Received from Friends Scale			
Friends give you advice on money matters	.02	.18	.05
Friends help you make a decision on a big purchase	-.11	.26*	-.12
Friends give you gifts	.15	-.26*	-.03
Help Received from Children Scale			
Children help you out with money	.05	.09	.17
	-.01	-.08	.20
	.00	.24*	.21

Table 11 (continued)

	Use Social Service Agencies	Number Perceived Formal Agencies as Helping Source	Number Agencies to Which Subjects Turned
Help Given to Children Scale			
Babysit grandchildren	.08	-.11	.15
Give advice on running a home and	-.05	.12	.27*
bringing up grandchildren	.16	-.12	.10
Subjects' Perception of Major Helping Source			
Turn to self	.12	-.36*	-.16
Turn to relatives	-.12	-.28*	-.01
Turn to friends	-.05	.08	.11
Visits a Group of Friends	-.05	-.03	.02

[a]Two subjects missing data on use of Social Service Agencies (N=46)

*p<.05   **p<.01

correlated with 2 self-help measures: friends give you advice on money matters ($r=.26$, $p<.05$) and children help you out with money ($r=.24$, $p<.05$). One self-help measure, babysit with grandchildren, was correlated with the number of agencies to which the subjects turned for help ($r=.27$, $p<.05$).

The number of situations where the subjects perceived formal agencies as the major source of help had negative correlations with 4 self-help measures. The strongest negative correlation was between number of situations in which the subjects perceived formal agencies as the major helping source and the number of situations when the subjects perceived themselves as the major helping source ($r=-.36$, $p<.01$). The number of situations when the subjects perceived formal agencies as the major helping source correlated negatively with: (1) number of DLA gone to with family ($r=-.29$, $p<.05$); (2) friends help you make a decision on a big purchase ($r=-.26$, $p<.05$); and (3) number of situations when relatives were perceived as the major helping source ($r=-.28$, $p<.05$).

The data indicated that no strong positive correlations existed between the subjects' use or non-use of social service agencies or between their perceptions of their need for social service agencies and the 17 self-help variables. However, negative correlations were revealed between the number of situations where the subjects perceived the formal agencies as the major helping source and situations when they perceived themselves as the major helping source. Negative correlations were also found between the subjects' perceptions of the formal agency as the major helping source and (1) number of Daily Life Activities (DLA) gone to with family; (2) friends help you make a decision on a big purchase; and (3) subjects turning to their relatives as the major helping source.

Thus, the older people apparently turned to social service agencies for the things they felt the informal system could not do for them, services which required extensive ongoing commitment or financial assistance that the informal network (including family) may have been either unable or unwilling to commit themselves to. Yet another situation where social service agencies became involved was the technical skill type (requiring information which the average family member or friend might not possess).

Katz and Bender, among others, indicated that the unique quality of human services was such that much of the work could be performed by people with no formal systematic knowledge or training. Their humaneness, feeling for people, caring, down-to-earth experience and common sense, availability and time enabled them to provide the appropriate help. Others, such as Sidel and Sidel and Gartner and Riessman, felt that some professional expertise was also required when technical-skill situations were involved. They, therefore, suggested that self-help groups could help professionals learn how to work more humanely with patients and clients.[21]

Self-Help With Formal Non-Senior Social Group Participation

Efforts were made to ascertain whether there was any relationship existing between the subjects' use of self-help and/or their perceptions of who their helping sources were and the subjects' participation in formal non-senior social groups which were not exclusively for the elderly (i.e., religious organizations, YW/YMHA, hiking clubs, Hadassah Women, political clubs, workmen benefit funds, and charitable organizations). The relationship between the 17 self-help measures and 4 formal non-senior social group participation measures were examined using Spearman rank-order correlation coefficients (see Table 12).

Religious organizations. Visits to religious organizations had moderately strong correlations with: (1) the subjects' perceptions of friends as a major source of help ($r=.50$, $p<.001$); (2) number of Daily Life Activities (DLA) to which the subjects did not go ($r=.32$, $p<.01$); (3) number of DLA gone to alone ($r=.33$, $p<.01$); and (4) friends give you advice on money matters ($r=.32$, $p<.01$). Visits to religious organizations had negative correlations with (1) number of DLA gone to with family ($r=-.28$, $p<.05$); (2) number of DLA gone to with friends ($r=-.37$, $p<.01$); (3) help-received-

Table 12
Spearman Rank-Order Correlation Coefficients for Relationships Between Seventeen Self-Help Measure and Four Formal Non-Senior Social Group Participation Measures (N = 48)

	Visits Religious Organizations	Visits Other Organizations	Number of Groups Visited	Visited Similar Groups in Earlier Life
Number of Daily Life Activities				
Don't go	.32**	-.18	-.17	.18
Go alone	.33**	-.07	.08	.16
Go with family	-.28*	.02	-.06	.01
Go with friends	-.37**	.16	-.04	-.26*
Help Received from Friends Scale	-.31*	.37**	.10	-.13
Friends give you advice on money matters	.32**	.34**	.25*	.00
Friends help you make a decision on a big purchase	-.13	-.13	.01	.01
Friends give you gifts	-.01	.08	.10	.06
Help Received from Children Scale	-.19	.06	.01	-.18
Children help you out with money	-.09	.24*	.03	-.14

Table 12 (continued)

	Visits Religious Organizations	Visits Other Organizations	Number of Groups Visited	Visited Similar Groups in Earlier Life
Help Given to Children Scale				
Babysit with grandchildren	.02	.15	.16	-.08
Give advice on running a home and	-.06	-.05	-.29*	-.09
bringing up grandchildren	.14	.11	.16	-.21
Subjects' Perceptions of Major Helping Sources				
Turn to self	-.20	.05	.03	-.09
Turn to relatives	-.30*	.20	-.05	-.11
Turn to friends	.50***	-.27*	.14	.11
Visits a group of friends	.11	.09	.53[3]	.13

*p<.05   **p<.01   ***p<.001

from friends scale ($r=-.31$, $p<.05$); and (4) the subjects' perceptions of relatives as a major helping source ($r=-.30$, $p<.05$). While visits to religious organizations had a moderately strong relationship to seeking advice or help from friends, it also appeared to either have a negative or nonexistent relationship to the other self-help measures. This was apparently an issue of personal belief unrelated to the subjects' use or non-use of the informal support system.

Other organizations. There were 3 positive and 1 negative correlations between visits other organizations and the self-help measures. Visits other organizations was moderately correlated with (1) the help-received-from-friends scale ($r=.37$, $p<.01$); (2) friends give you advice on money matters ($r=.34$, $p<.01$); and (3) children help you out with money ($r=.24$, $p<.05$). The one negative correlation concerned the subjects' perceptions of friends as a major helping source ($r=-.27$, $p<.05$). The data showed that visits to other organizations (e.g., lodges, YW/YMHA's, hiking clubs, fraternal organizations, Hadassah Women, and political clubs) was basically related to the friends variables. Thus, these organizations appeared to be groups where one participated and interacted with friends; therefore, it would have been natural to seek help from friends among these groups.

Number of groups visited. This variable correlated strongly with one self-help variable--visits a group of friends ($r=.53$, $p<.001$). It was also correlated with friends give you advice on money matters ($r=.25$, $p<.05$) and correlated negatively with babysit for grandchildren ($r=-.29$, $p<.05$). Again number of groups visited correlated most strongly with visits with a group of friends. This outcome was predictable, since visiting non-senior citizens organizations tended to be activities participated in with friends. The act that some subjects spent time babysitting may have meant that they did not have much discretionary time for visiting organizations or participating in group activities.

Earlier life activities. Only one self-help measure correlated negatively with visited similar groups in earlier life: number of Daily Life Activities (DLA) gone to with friends

($r = -.26$, $p < .05$). Perhaps the subjects' participation in similar groups during an earlier period had little or no bearing on their current interactions or involvement in DLA or on their interactions with families and friends. The data do seem to indicate that those who participated in similar groups during earlier periods do not currently go with friends to the DLA.

Of the formal non-senior social group measures which correlated positively with the self-help measures, the strongest relationships involved support from, or interaction with, friends. The friends self-help measures for this group did not include escort services or going places together, but rather involved the elderly turning to them for help under various circumstances. However, when looking at the nature of the other organizations (i.e., lodges, YW/YMHA, hiking clubs, fraternal organizations, Hadassah Women, political clubs, workmen benefit funds, and charitable organizations) these clearly were organizations where one was likely to participate and interact with friends or at least peers and colleagues. Therefore, it would have been natural to seek help from friends among these groups. Furthermore, the members probably had interests similar to the subjects.

The subjects who visited religious organizations perceived friends as their major source of help and took advice from their friends on money matters; however, these subjects went alone to the Daily Life Activities (DLA) or not at all. The negative relationships between visits religious organizations and go with friends and family to DLA would seem to suggest that those subjects who visited religious organizations did not go to any of the DLA with friends or family members. Possibly, the subjects who visited religious organizations were single respondents without children or close relatives; all of the positive relationships were with friends or self-dependent.

The number of groups visited had its strongest correlations with visits with a group of friends indicating that the subjects visited more groups when accompanied by friends. No relationship existed between subjects who participated in similar groups during earlier periods and current involvement or interactions. However, the data did indicate that their earlier participation was unrelated to the places they currently went with friends.

The four variables above and the elderly's use of social services seemed unrelated. In other words, whether or not the subjects participated in the formal non-senior citizens' social group activities had no apparent bearing on their use or non-use of formal social service agencies. One may infer, therefore, that the subjects visited the 4 non-senior social groups to fulfill their expressive or ideological needs. The use of social service agencies supported needs which were more instrumental in nature.

The Correlation Among Different Self-Help Activities

The data were analyzed to determine whether or not there was any correlation between the actual use of the various self-help activities. The self-help measures were examined, using Spearman rank-order correlations coefficients, for relationships between pairs of the self-help measures (see Appendix M).

Positive correlations--behavior to behavior. The 2 strongest pairs of positive relationships among the self-help measures were between help given to children and help received from children ($r=.69$, $p<.001$) and help received from friends and go with friends to the 12 Daily Life Activities (DLA) ($r=.64$, $p<.001$). There were also positive correlations between the elderly subjects' babysitting grandchildren and the help-received-from-children scale ($r=.27$, $p<.05$) (see Appendix M). These relationships indicated that reciprocity existed in the relationships between the elderly and their children and between them and their friends. As mentioned earlier in the chapter, Wentowski found that the basic cultural rule for reciprocity was "for something received, something had to be given in return."[22] She also discovered that if this rule were not obeyed, participants in the process would eventually withdraw from the exchange. This rule allowed the elderly persons to maintain as much of their independence as possible, given their resources.

The Correlations Between the Subjects' Perceptions of Helping Sources, e.g., Self, Relatives and Friends

The data were analyzed to determine the relationship between the elderly subjects' perceptions of helping sources (e.g., self, relatives, and friends) and their actual participation in the self-help activities using the Spearman rank-order correlation coefficient (see Appendix N).

Correlations between behavior and attitude. The strongest positive correlations between the subjects' perceptions concerning who would be the most likely person to provide assistance under various circumstances and the subjects' actual behavior were related to the two friends variables, namely, their perceptions of friends as the major helping source and visits with a group of friends. The visits with a group of friends correlated positively with: (1) the help-received-from-friends scale ($r=.30$, $p<.05$); (2) go with friends to the Daily Life Activities (DLA) ($r=.28$, $p<.05$); and (3) perception of friends as the major helping source ($r=.26$, $p<.05$). Perception of friends as the major helping source also correlated positively with friends help with a decision regarding a big purchase ($r=.29$, $p<.05$) (see Appendix N). Thus, the data show that the elderly who are oriented to the friendship network do, in fact, use it.

Two positive correlations were found for the perception of relatives as the major helping source: (1) go with family to the DLA ($r=.28$, $p<.05$); and (2) the elderly babysitting their grandchildren ($r=.26$, $p<.05$) (see Appendix N.) These correlations supported the previous observation of reciprocity between the elderly and their children.

Negative correlations of behavior with attitude. The strongest negative correlations were between the elderly subjects' perceptions of friends as the major helping source and their perception of relatives as the major helping source ($r=-.61$, $p<.001$). There were negative correlations for perception of friends as the major helping source with: (1) go with family to the DLA ($r=-.36$, $p<.01$); and (2) perception of themselves as the major helping source ($r=-.33$, $p<.01$).

Negative correlations existed between visits group of friends and don't go to the DLA ($r=-.34$, $p<.01$). The negative relationship between the friends variables and family variables further suggested that those subjects who depended more heavily on their families did not interact much with friends and vice-versa.

However, the data do support the contention that friends and family could have been depended on, but under different circumstances. The latter possibility is supported by Litwak et al. who suggested that primary groups could provide support and/or help with tasks which more readily fit their structure.[23] In the present study the subjects perceived family members and friends as helping them equally but with different things. Family members assisted with activities related to long-term commitment, but did not require constant close proximity while friends assisted with activities which were "affective" or social in nature as well as activities which required close proximity.

Now that the findings of this study have been presented in Chapter IV, let us turn to the concluding chapter, Chapter V.

Notes

1. Cantor reported from her study of the "Inner City Elderly" that subjects in that research defined the neighborhood as having a maximum radius of 10 city blocks. That definition has been accepted for the purpose of this study. Marjorie H. Cantor, "Life Space and the Social Support Systems of the Inner City Elderly of New York" (paper presented to the Gerontological Society, Miami Beach, Florida, November 8, 1973).

2. Ibid., 8.

3. Eugene Litwak, in collaboration with John Dono, Cecilia Falbe, Barbara Kail, Steve Kulis, Sam Marullo and Roger Sherman, "The Modified Extended Family, Social Networks, and Research Continuities in Aging," Monograph 73, 1981, prepared for a University Seminar, Duke University, Durham, North Carolina; Marjorie H. Cantor, "The Formal and Informal Social Support System of Older New Yorkers," paper presented at Symposium: The City a Viable Environment for the Elderly?" (10th International Congress of Gerontology, Jerusalem, Israel, June 1975); and Gloria J. Wentowski, "Reciprocity and the Coping Strategies of Older People: Cultural Dimensions of Network Building," *The Gerontologist*, 21, no. 6 (1981).

4. Mary J. Mayer, "Kin and Neighbors: Differential Roles in Differing Cultures," (paper presented at 29th Annual Gerontological Society Meeting, New York, October 1976), 4; and Cantor, "The Formal and Informal Social Support System of Older New Yorkers," 4.

5. Frances J. Dory, *Building Self-Help Groups Among Older Persons* (New York: New Careers Training Laboratory, Graduate School and University Center, CUNY, 1979); Solomon Katz, "Anthropological Perspective on Aging," *The Annuals of the American Academy of Political and Social Science*, July 1978; Joseph A. Califano, "The Aging of America: Questions for a Four Generation

Society," 96-108; Judith Treas, "Family Support Systems for the Aged: Some Social and Demographic Considerations," in *The Age of Aging, A Reader in Social Gerontology,* ed. Abraham Monk, 1979; and Abraham Monk, "Family Supports in Old Age," *Social Work,* 24, no. 7 (1976).

6.   Helen Z. Lopata, "Social Relations of Widows in Black and White Communities" (U.S. Department of Health, Education and Welfare, Social Rehabilitation Services, 1965), 39.

7.   Wentowski, "Reciprocity and the Coping Strategies of Older People," 605; Mayer, "Kin and Neighbors," 4; Cantor, "The Formal and Informal Social Support System of Older New Yorkers," 6; and Ruby Banks Abrahams, "Mutual Help for the Widowed," *Social Work,* 17, no. 5 (September 1972): 54-61.

8.   The response categories for the items in the scales in Appendices G, H, and I are recoded to (1) not at all; (2) only occasionally; (3) fairly often, and (4) very often.

9.   It should be underscored that this study focused on the activities and interactions of the "well aged" and that this focus probably accounted for the above findings.

10.   Mayer, "Kin and Neighbors," 4; and Cantor, "The Formal and Informal Social Support System of Older New Yorkers," 6.

11.   Wentowski, "Reciprocity and the Coping Strategies of Older People," 605.

12.   The ten situations included: (1) you suddenly feel sick or dizzy; (2) you want to talk to someone about a problem concerning your child or someone else in your family; (3) you need to borrow a few dollars until your next check comes; (4) you feel lonely and want to talk; (5) you need a new light bulb in the ceiling; (6) you need someone to help you get to the doctor; (7) you find you do not have enough money to cover a very big medical bill; (8) you are in the hospital and need someone to look after your apartment; (9) you need someone to help you fill out a form; and (10) you have an accident and

need someone to come in each day to bathe and help you take your medicine.

13. Social service agencies will be analyzed as an independent variable later in this chapter (see page 57).

14. Eugene Litwak, in collaboration with John Dono, Cecilia Falhe, Barbara Kail, Steve Kuhn, Sam Marullo, and Roger Sherman, "The Modified Extended Family, Social Networks, and Research Continuities in Aging," Monograph 73, 12.

15. The six group classifications are: Close friends, neighbors, kin-children and other relatives, spouses, "no one" and formal organizations--which include all people who are paid for their help. For further discussion regarding the empirical findings relating to this structure; see ibid., 12-36.

16. Marjorie H. Cantor and Mary J. Mayer, "Factors in Differential Utilization of Services by Urban Elderly" (paper presented at 28th Annual Scientific Meeting of the Gerontological Society, Louisville, Kentucky, 1975), 6.

17. Lopata, "Social Relations of Widows in Black and White Communities," 39; and New York State Office for Aging, *Family Caregiving and the Elderly: Policy Recommendations and Research Findings,* March 1983, 12.

18. Susan R. Sherman, "Mutual Assistance and Support in Retirement Housing," *Journal of Gerontology,* 30, no. 4 (1975): 482.

19. Wentowski, "Reciprocity and the Coping Strategies of Older People," 603.

20. Informal discussions with the staff of the Far Rockaway center revealed that many of the trips engaged in by the elderly in that center were planned by the center staff.

21. Alfred Katz and Eugene Bender, *The Strength in Us, Self-Help Groups in the Modern World* (New York: New Viewpoint, a Division of Franklin Watts, 1976), 8; Frank Riessman and Alan Gartner, *Self-Help in the Human Services* (San Francisco: Jossey Bass, Inc., Publishers, 1977), 9; and Victor Sidel and Ruth Sidel, "Beyond Coping," *Social Policy,* September/October 1976, 68.

22. Wentowski, "Reciprocity and the Coping Strategies of Older People," 602-603.

23. Litwak et al., "The Modified Extended Family, Social Networks, and Research Continuities in Aging," 12-36.

V
SUMMARY, DISCUSSION, CONCLUSIONS, IMPLICATIONS, AND RECOMMENDATIONS

SUMMARY OF SELF-HELP

The goal of this study was to provide information on the role of self-help among the elderly and, at the same time, provide evidence of the continuing need for formalized social services. As seen in previous chapters, the study showed the following: (1) reciprocal help between the elderly and their children; (2) the interactions between the elderly and their friends (including, neighbors and social activity group members) and help provided by their friends; (3) the relationship between the demographic characteristics of the elderly and their interaction with family to patterns of self-help activities; (4) the relationship between the mobility of the subjects and their participation in self-help activities; and finally (5) the correlation between the subjects' perceptions of helping sources (e.g., self, friends, relatives, or social agencies) and actual use of the self-help activities.

Reciprocity Between Parents and Children

As documented throughout the literature, there is widespread reciprocity between older persons and their children. The two areas in this study where reciprocity existed most frequently were gift giving (60 percent), and crisis intervention or help when someone was ill (32 percent) (see Table 13). There were other categories where help was provided by parents to children and vice-versa; however, the reciprocity for the same tasks is minimal. This did not preclude the possibility of exchanges taking place in different areas (e.g., a child may have shopped or run errands for a parent and, in return, the parent could have helped out with money).

Interaction Between the Elderly and Friends

The elderly interacted with and received help from their friends in three areas. The first area was escort to social activities which required public transportation and took the elderly outside of the neighborhood. The data here indicated that the activities outside of the neighborhood in which the elderly engaged most frequently were social (e.g., movie/theater 58 percent, and bar/restaurants 50 percent), except for visits to the doctor or clinic and clothes shopping.

The second area was related to "affective" help or social support. In a scale ranging from a high of 4 to a low of 1, the elderly depended upon their friends to "provide conversation" for a mean score of 3.00. They visited with each other for a mean of 2.3 times and went on trips together half of the times. When the elderly were asked to whom they would turn for help under certain circumstances, they indicated that they would turn to friends if they felt lonely and wanted to talk.

Finally, the third area was response to emergency situations. In emergency situations, the elderly indicated, their friends were the most likely persons to whom they would turn.

Impact of Demographic Characteristics on Self-help

The elderly subjects in this study most likely to participate in self-help activities were the older members of the group. These subjects gave and received more help from their children than the younger members. They had no spouses, but did have living children with whom they interacted fairly regularly (at least monthly). These gave a great deal more to their children than the married subjects; in fact, the exchanges between parent and children were about equal.

The subjects of this study were predominately female and Jewish. A Mann-Whitney U Test indicated that male subjects were less likely to participate in Daily Life Activities (DLA) than the females. The

Table 13
Frequencies for Reciprocity in Self-Help Activities Between the Elderly and Their Children (N=48)

Daily Life Activities	Children-Parent		Parent-Children		Children-Parent	
	f	*%*	*f*	*%*	*f*	*%*
Give gifts	31	64.6	33	68.8	29	60.4
Help out when someone is ill	21	47.7	18	40.9	14	31.8
Shop or run errands	19	40.4	4	8.5	2	4.3
Fix things around the house	12	25.5	2	4.3	1	2.1
Help out with money	1	2.1	12	25.5	0	--
Help make a decision on a big purchase, such as a car	9	19.6	1	2.2	1	2.2
Keep house	1	2.2	1	2.2	1	2.2

Jewish subjects were more likely than the non-Jewish subjects to participate in the DLA along with another person and their level of receiving help from friends was higher. These elderly subjects were also among the better educated. The data showed that the more educated subjects interacted with, and provided help to, their families more frequently than the less educated. Contrastingly, the data showed that the less educated elderly subjects perceived their friends as their greatest helping sources.

The Relationship Between Mobility and Self-Help

When mobility was examined to determine if distance traveled and use of different modes of transportation had any impact on use of various helping sources, it was found that these variables related more strongly to assistance from friends. The activities relating to DLA to which the elderly traveled the greatest distance to visit via public transportation were social or recreational in nature, except for visits to the doctor or clinic, to which they most often traveled alone. These also were the activities to which friends were chosen to accompany the elderly more frequently.

The subjects, as stated above, depended primarily upon themselves to get to the doctor or clinic; also, to the bank, drugstore, grocery store and clubs or organizations (see Table 14). Of the five activities to which they went alone, the doctor or clinic was the only activity traveled to more frequently outside of the neighborhood which under any circumstances required some form of transportation. Help received from relatives did not appear to affect the mobility of the subjects very much except for receiving help from children, which did appear to impact negatively upon whether or not the subjects traveled within the neighborhood to the DLA. Family members did not provide the largest percentage of any escort services, however; they matched the "alone" category for clothes shopping (25 percent) (see Table 14), and the "friends" category for escorting the subjects to the grocery store (23 percent). They provided the second highest percentage of escort to the doctor or clinic--the largest percentage of subjects (65 percent) went alone to the doctor or clinic.

Table 14
Frequencies for Sources of Escorts to the Daily Life Activities (N = 8)

Daily Life Activities	Sources of Escort			
	Family %	Friends %	Alone %	Don't Go %
Grocery store	23	23	48	6
Butcher	15	18	25	42
Drugstore	15	15	54	16
Doctor/clinic	21	4	65	10
Clothing store	25	23	25	27
Church/synagogue	17	8	31	44
Bank	17	19	56	8
Park	6	2	13	79
Movie/theater	17	44	10	29
Club/organization	2	34	44	20
Job/business	--	--	--	100
Bar/restaurant	13	44	8	35

Perception of Helping Sources

As suggested by Litwak, Cantor, Mayer, and others, the present study also found that the most important categories of helping among elderly subjects were from neighbors and friends in emergency situations. In addition to the socialization activities which were important to the elderly-friends' relationship, the data revealed that the majority of the elderly turned to friends for emergency assistance (see Table 15) or close proximity-type activities (e.g., sudden illness or loneliness or someone to look after the apartment while in the hospital). For other needs, the elderly subjects turned to self, family and friends almost equally (e.g., to talk to someone about a problem concerning a family member). They depended equally upon themselves and family for emergency funds, and depended upon family members first, then a social agency, for help in paying major medical bills. Formal social agency help was clearly preferred in two areas: help with household repairs and extended, skilled nursing care.

CONCLUSIONS

The study findings provided data to support the existence of self-help among the two groups studied and their use of formal social service agencies. The data focused on four sources of help: (1) friends (including neighbors and social activity group members); (2) family (the majority of the information gathered concerned help provided by children); (3) the things the elderly depended on themselves to do; and (4) services provided by formal agencies (including social service agencies). The data also showed the elderly reciprocated with help to their children.

Reciprocity in Self-help Activities Between the Elderly and Their Children

Several researchers on self-help for the elderly, including Abrahams, Cantor, Mayer, and Wentowski, have maintained that family members have always interacted with, and provided varying types of support for, their elderly kin. These writers also have suggested that a mutual exchange occurred between the elderly and their kin. The data from the present study supported this conclusion.

Table 15
Frequencies for Sources of Help, i.e., Family, Friends, Social Agency, and Self (N=48)

					Perceptions of Helping Sources			
						Social		
	Family		Friends		Agency		Self	
Daily Life Activities	f	%	f	%	f	%	f	%
a. You suddenly feel sick or dizzy	12	25	29	60	2	4	5	10
b. You want to talk to someone abouat a problem concerning your child or someone else in your family	14	29	13	27	7	15	14	29
c. You need to borrow a few dollars until your next check comes	17	35	12	25	2	4	17	35
d. You feel lonely and want to talk	9	19	30	63	2	4	7	15
e. You need a new light bulb in the ceiling	3	6	6	13	26	54	13	27
f. You need someone to help you get to the doctor	13	27	15	31	14	29	6	13
g. You find you do not have enough money to cover a very big medical bill	18	38	2	4	16	33	12	25
h. You are in the hospital and need someone to look after your apartment	19	40	22	46	2	4	5	10
i. You need someone to help you fill out a form	8	17	7	15	12	25	21	14
j. You have an accident and need someone to come in each day to bathe and help you take your medicine	14	29	7	15	25	52	2	4

Code: 1 + 2 = Self
      3 + 4 = Family
      5 + 6 + 8 = Friends
      7 + 9 = Formal agency

Here, most of the subjects lived within the metropolitan New York City area. Those subjects with children had at least one child who contacted them weekly by telephone and saw them at least monthly.

The elderly received help from their children and in return provided help to them. The highest level of exchange between subjects and children was gift-giving; the frequency of exchange was almost equal but was slightly higher for the elderly. The next highest level of exchange was helping out during illness; the children provided slightly more help. These results were consistent with Mayer and Cantor's findings in their separate reports of the data from the study of inner-city elderly.[1] These results were also true for Wentowski who found that "most of the elderly had one or more relatives on whom they could depend."[2]

Wentowski established that 70 percent of them had significant exchange with one or more children. In the present study, the strongest relationship existing in the exchange network was between the elderly and their children.

A relatively high negative correlation existed between using the family as escort to Daily Life Activities (DLA) and using friends (see Appendix M). A strong negative correlation also existed between the perception of friends as the major helping source and family members as the major helping source. One could surmise that the subjects who depended on relatives did not have interactions with friends and vice-versa. However, the data also give credence to the possibility that the subjects interacted with and depended upon both, but used them under different circumstances. This possibility is supported by Litwak who suggested that primary groups could provide and/or help with tasks which matched their structure.[3] The preference for using friends over family for escort services as well as the subjects' suggesting them as the major helping source could perhaps be explained by the fact that some of the subjects indicated that most of their children lived outside the metropolitan area (see Appendix K)--making it difficult for them to be readily available to provide these services.

Interaction Between the Elderly and Their Friends

Among the study aims was the gathering of information on: (1) the support and assistance the friends of the elderly provided; (2) the use of friends as escorts; and (3) whether or not the elderly belonged to groups involving friends. Not specifically addressed was the question of whether or not the elderly returned favors for their friends. However, based upon general knowledge about the strong sense of independence among this group, supported throughout the literature, one could hypothesize that the same type of reciprocity existing between the elderly and their children also existed with their friends. If correct, then the level of reciprocity between many of the elderly and their friends is equally as high as that existing between them and their children. However, no empirical data were gathered to support this hypothesis.

Friends supplied the greatest support for the elderly in, respectively, providing conversation for them, visiting with them, and going with them on trips. In Cantor's study,[4] these activities related to socialization and were deemed to have significant importance to the elderly in the neighborhood. For the elderly in this study, the socialization process extended beyond the immediate neighborhood with staff assistance from the two social activity centers (e.g., the staff members of the two social activity centers assisted in arranging and facilitating many of the trips to restaurants, movies/theater, and shopping centers outside of the neighborhood). The subjects indicated that on these trips they usually went with a friend.

When visits to other organizations (e.g. lodges, YW/YMHA, hiking clubs, fraternal organizations, and charitable organizations) were looked at, strong correlations existed with help-the-elderly-received-from-friends variables, including friends giving them advice on money matters. Since one would routinely participate and interact with friends in this context, it would be natural for those subjects who participated to seek help from friends in these groups. The elderly who visited religious organizations also perceived their friends as a major helping source.

The elderly who depended on friends to help tended to rely on them as escorts a great deal. Those who received help from friends and went with friends to DLA did not go to many if help or an escort were unavailable (see Appendix M). Those who went with friends did not go with family members, suggesting that the elderly who were oriented to the friendship network did, indeed use it.

Demographic Characteristics of the Elderly and Self-Help

When the demographic data were scrutinized, it was determined that older subjects who were unmarried but had living children participated more frequently in the exchange process than younger subjects, who were likely to be married. The literature indicated that the spouse was the normal first source of help.[5] Here, too, the married subjects, who were also the younger subjects, tended to depend more on the spouse for the exchange of support. The subjects who participated alone in activities most frequently were the single, non-Jewish subjects without children. One study suggested that the elderly, like most people, tend to continue the patterns developed over a lifetime.[6] In the present study, it was suggested that these subjects developed a pattern of independence over the years and continued it.

The most educated subjects interacted with others, providing help to them more frequently. One could hypothesize that the most educated subjects were likely to have had better jobs which provided higher incomes, enabling them to accumulate more resources to participate in activities with friends as well as provide service exchange. Unfortunately, the income variable could not be analyzed; thus, there were no empirical data to support this hypothesis (see Chapter III for explanation).

Mobility and self-help. Some Daily Life Activities (DLA) in which the elderly subjects engaged were located within the neighborhood (e.g., clubs/organizations, grocery stores, church/synagogue,and the bank) and could be performed alone. There were other DLA, basically socialization activities, for which they used public transportation to travel outside of the neighborhood. These activities were performed with friends as well as with assistance from the two social activity centers. There was, however, one DLA to which the subjects traveled outside of the neighborhood alone, using public transportation, namely, visits to the doctor or clinic. The inaccessibility of medical services to the elderly was discussed by Cantor as a contributing factor preventing inner-city and middle-class older people from getting vital medical services as frequently as needed.[7] Data from the present study indicated that only 22 percent of the elderly turned to social service agencies during the year prior to the survey.

The two agencies turned to were senior centers (33 percent) and the social security office (27 percent). The elderly reported that they turned to their friends and families more frequently than to social service agencies; when they did turn to a social service agency, it was to request help with skilled medical care and extended or ongoing medical care. Perhaps assisting the elderly with transportation to medical care is an area where social service agencies--including senior centers--could move more aggressively to fill the gap through coordinating informal escort services already available to the elderly as well as instituting additional transportation services.

In regard to whom the subjects turned for assistance under varying circumstances, generally the data supported the division-of-tasks structure for the primary network presented by Litwak et al.[8] Using friends for support in an emergency medical situation or a normal social situation related to the need for close proximity but not necessarily long-term commitment. In addition, the choice of friends for free-time activities supported their findings as well. The areas where the subjects elected to accomplish a task themselves, e.g., filling out forms, or securing emergency cash, were also consistent with the other studies' findings. However, contrary to those findings, in this study a social agency was chosen by the highest percentage of subjects for home care when ill as opposed to kin; friends were chosen as the persons whom they would talk to when they felt lonely as opposed to kin. Differences between the two studies could relate to the different periods when they were conducted or different locations.

IMPLICATIONS OF FINDINGS

Public policy development as well as social service planning for the elderly are encompassed by the present study. Clearly the elderly, as well as people of all ages, tend to prefer help from relatives and friends rather than social agencies. Not surprisingly, the elderly are strong believers in reciprocity as per Wentowski. Others, including Litwak and Cantor, have pointed out that formal agencies retain specific roles.

Planning of Services for Elderly

Social agencies assess an older person on the basis of determining future needs. Built into any assessment should be: (1) some determination of what resources exist in the informal network to help a person; (2) an investigation of which older persons are willing to use the network; and (3) how the social worker could facilitate the process before turning to the formal agency (e.g a nursing home). The availability of the informal network (e.g., relatives and friends) should be examined in order to determine what the social worker might do to mobilize the network's response to an older person's needs. Greater emphasis should be placed on the social worker and other helping professionals (e.g., nurses and mental health workers) acting as brokers and managers of services for the older person. In order to perform these roles effectively, they should acquire comprehensive knowledge of the older people with whom they are dealing--including awareness of the availability of informal networks as well as the elderly person's perception of, and comfort in, using the network.

More accessible transportation to medical care for the elderly is another area where the social agency could play a more productive role. As early as 1973, Cantor suggested that alternative means of transportation were urgently needed in order for the elderly to receive adequate medical care.[9] While some alternatives to public transportation are available (e.g., privately owned and operated ambulettes and invalid buses), these are usually coordinated through the provider of medical services for medicaid patients only. Senior activity centers, for example, have ongoing contacts with the able bodied elderly and could coordinate already-available informal escort services as well as formal agency-provided transportation. This would help all elderly, especially the frail, to receive the needed care.

Public Policy Implications

Public policy implications here relate to the current emphasis by the federal government on the informal network (e.g. family members), as public support for social needs is increasingly withdrawn. The federal government's data on help-seeking patterns of older persons may be inadequate. Furthermore, the present study would seem to suggest that volunteerism is a mutually supportive structure, not a replacement for services by formal agency. While it is most assuredly important to be sensitive to the values and strengths of the informal network, it could be very damaging to older people's survival to assume that the informal network can replace the formal.

In addition, even though the older person may usually prefer the informal network, a clear preference exists for the social agency to provide specific services (e.g., extended skilled health care and financial aid for meeting exorbitant medical bills). Based upon the current cost of medical services, it is not difficult to understand why older persons would not always prefer the informal network. However, given the decreasing government allowances and reimbursement for these services, older persons might well elect to forego badly needed care--thus sacrificing their ability to live extended, healthy lives in their own communities near their families, friends and neighbors.

RECOMMENDATIONS FOR FUTURE RESEARCH

Inadequate research often has been blamed for the paucity of data concerning self-help activities such as the nature and extent of professional involvement in the functioning of self-help or the motivation of group members. Other observers have felt that disciplined investigation in self-help groups remains a novelty: "Little useful information exists about what factors in society determine the emergence of self-help groups and why people join them."[10]

Killilea suggested that there is need for intensive case studies of specific groups and for surveys of different kinds of mutual help organizations locally, regionally, and nationally.[11]

While systematic studies on self-help groups certainly have not been plentiful, the literature on the subject has grown. Indeed, self-help resources range from providing emotional support for a bereaved widow or widower to helping a new immigrant and providing supplemental supportive social services for a neighbor or friend. Many such activities are informal, one-on-one endeavors or small group support, such as a neighbor or community group; some groups are formally organized and assisted by professionals. More research is needed on the role of the self-help network exchange, especially as it relates to the older population and the extent to which members utilize it. The following are recommended:

1. Survey items that provide information on the informal reciprocity network of the elderly should be included in a major survey such as the U.S. Census, or other national surveys which draw on national representation. Variables should permit a large cross-section

(e.g., age, ethnicity, socioeconomic status, and number of children) of elderly to participate.

2. Research should include a quality-of-life survey focusing on the well-being of network participants. The survey results could be useful in developing a typology of the elderly engaged in the reciprocity networks.

3. Research should be conducted to identify the elderly who do not participate in any network. These elderly should be compared to those who do in order to determine whether or not the quality of life is, in fact, richer for the participants. This research also should help to determine whether formal services can be substituted for the informal network.

4. Research should be conducted to determine that the extent to which the elderly engage in the self-help network; questions which should be answered include: (1) whether or not the popular belief that many elderly are too dependent to engage in self-help networks is valid; (2) younger elderly whether or not feel a need for support networks; or (3) whether or not there has been sufficient study to determine the true extent to which the elderly engage in self-help network exchange.

Research designed to address the above concerns will assist in policy development and service planning to aid the growing population of elderly, allowing them to live healthy, productive lives in their communities near their families, friends and neighbors. As pointed out by previous researchers on programs for the elderly, older people have a strong need to remain independent and to participate as equals in the exchange process. Programs and services which facilitate this need will affect positively the quality of life for this growing population. Assisting in achieving this objective has been the aim of this study.

Notes

1. Mary Mayer, "Kin and Neighbors: Differential Roles in Differing Cultures" (paper presented at 29th Annual Gerontological Society Meeting, New York, October, 1976), 4; and Marjorie H. Cantor, "The Formal and Informal Social Support System of Older New Yorkers" (paper presented at the 10th International Congress of Gerontology, Jerusalem, Israel, June 25, 1975), 6.

2. Gloria Wentowski, "Reciprocity and the Coping Strategies of Older People: Cultural Dimensions of Network Building," *The Gerontologist*, 21, no. 6 (1981): 600-609.

3. Eugene Litwak, *Helping the Elderly: The Complementary Roles of Informal Networks and Formal Systems* (New York: Guilford Press, 1985). (See chapter 3.)

4. Cantor, "The Formal and Informal Social Support System of Older New Yorkers," 8.

5. New York State Office for the Aging, *Family Caregiving and the Elderly; Policy Recommendations and Research Findings* (March 1983), 12.

6. Beth Hess, "Self-Help Among the Aged," *Social Policy*, 7, no. 3 (November/December 1976): 55.

7. Marjorie H. Cantor, "Life Space and the Social Support System of the Inner City Elderly of New York" (symposium: "The City: A Viable Environment for Older People," 26th Annual Meeting, Gerontological Society, Miami Beach, Florida, 1973), 21.

8. Litwak, *Helping the Elderly*, 12.

9. Cantor, "Life Space and the Social Support System of the Inner City Elderly of New York," 21.

10.   Naomi Curtis, ed., *Self-Help Reporter*, 3, no. 1 (January/February 1979): 1; Alfred H. Katz and Eugene I. Bender, *The Strength in Us: Self-Help Groups in the Modern World* (New York: New Viewpoint, a Division of Franklin Watz, 1976), 8; Alfred H. Katz, "Self-Help Organizations and Volunteer Participation in Social Welfare," *Social Work*, no. 15 (January 1970): 51-60; and Morton H. Lieberman, Leonard D. Borman, and Associates, *Self-Help Groups for Coping with Crisis* (San Francisco: Jossey-Bass Publishers, 1979), 1.

11.   Maria Killilea, "Mutual Help Organizations: Interpretations in Literature," in *Support Systems and Mutual Help: Multidisciplinary Explorations*, ed. Gerald Caplan and Maria Killilea (New York: Grune and Straton, Inc., 1976), 37-38.

BIBLIOGRAPHY

Abrahams, Ruby Banks. "Mutual Help for the Widowed." *Social Work*, 17, no. 5 (September 1972): 54-61.

Allen, Carole, and Herman Brotman. *The 1981 White House Conference of Aging, Chartbook on Aging in America.*

"Alone, Yearning for Companionship in America." *The New York Times Magazine*, August 15, 1982.

Annals of the American Academy of Political and Social Science, 438 (July 1978).

Armstrong, M. Jocelyn, and Karen S. Goldsteen. "Friendship Support Patterns of Older American Women." *Journal of Aging Studies*, 4, no. 4 (1990): 391-404.

Baker, Frank. "The Interface Between Professional and Natural Support Systems." *Clinical Social Work Journal*, 5, no. 2 (1977): 139-148.

Biegel, David E., Arthur J. Naparstek, and Mohammed M. Khan, eds. *Community Support Systems and Mental Health Practice, Policy and Research.* New York: Springer Publishing Company, 1982.

Binstock, Robert H., and Ethel Shanas. *Handbook of Aging and the Social Sciences.* New York: Van Nostrand Reinhold Company, Litton Educational Publishing Company, 1976.

Borman, Leonard D., Leslie E. Borck, Robert Hess, and Frank L. Pasquale, eds. *The Prevention in Human Services: Helping People to Help Themselves, Self-Help and Prevention.* Vol. 1, No. 3. New York: The Haworth Press, 1982.

Bowles, Elinor. "Older Persons as Providers of Services: Three Federal Programs." *Social Policy,* 7, no. 3 (November/December 1976): 81-88.

Brody, Elaine M. "The Aging Family." *The Gerontologist,* 6, no. 4 (December 1969): 201-206.

Bury, Michael, and Anthea Holme. "Quality of Life and Social Support in the Very Old." *Journal of Aging Studies,* 4, no. 4 (1990): 345-357.

Cantor, Marjorie H. "Life Space and the Social Support System of the Inner City Elderly of New York." Paper presented to "Symposium: The City: A Viable Environment for Older People?," 26th Annual Meeting of the Gerontological Society, Miami Beach, Florida, November 1973.

Cantor, Marjorie H. "The Formal and Informal Social Support System of Older New Yorkers." Paper presented at Symposium: "The City: A Viable Environment for the Elderly?," 10th International Congress of Gerontology, Jerusalem, Israel, June 1975.

Cantor, Marjorie H., and Mary J. Mayer. "Factors in Differential Utilization of Services by Urban Elderly." Paper presented at 28th Annual Scientific Meeting of the Gerontological Society, Louisville, Kentucky, October 1975.

Caplan, Gerald, and Marie Killilea, eds. *Support Systems and Mutual Help: Multidisciplinary Explorations.* New York: Grunt and Stratton, Inc., 1976.

Curtis, Naomi, ed. *Self-Help Reporter.* Vol. 3, No. 1. New York: National Self-Help Clearinghouse, Graduate School and University Center/CUNY, 1979.

Dory, Frances Jemmott. *Building Self-Help Groups Among Older Persons.* New York: New Careers Training Laboratory, Center for Advanced Study in Education, Graduate School and University Center/CUNY, 1979.

Dowd, James J. "Aging as Exchange: A Preface to Theory." *Journal of Gerontology*, 30, no. 5 (1975): 584-595.

Dowd, James J. *Stratification Among the Aged*. Monterey, CA: Brooks/Cole Publication Company, a division of Wadsworth, Inc. 1980.

Faulkner, Audrey O., and Marcel A. Heisel. "Giving, Receiving, and Exchanging: Elderly Blacks and Their Informal Support Systems." Paper presented at the 30th Annual Meeting of the Gerontological Society, 1977.

Finlayson, Angela. "Social Networks as Coping Resources: Lay Help and Consultation Patterns Used by Women in Husband's Post-Infraction Career." *Journal of Social Science and Medicine*, 10, no. 2 (February 1976): 97-103

Gartner, Alan, and Frank Riessman. *Self-Help in the Human Services*. San Francisco: Jossey-Bass, Inc., 1977.

Gartner, Alan, and Frank Reissman, eds. *The Self-Help Revolution*. New York: Human Science Press, 1984.

Gouldner, Alvin. "The Norm of Reciprocity: A Preliminary Statement." *American Sociological Review*, 25, no. 2 (April 1960): 161-178.

Gussow, Zachary, and George S. Tracy. "The Role of Self-Help Clubs in Adaptation to Chronic Illness and Disability." *Journal of Social Science and Medicine*, 10, no. 7/8 (1976): 407-414.

Haas, J. Eugene, and Thomas E. Drabek. *Complex Organizations: A Sociological Perspective*. New York: MacMillan Publishing Company, Inc., 1973.

Hess, Beth B. *Growing Old in America*. New Brunswick, N.J.: Transactions Books, 1976.

Hess, Beth B. Self-Help Among the Aged." *Social Policy*, 7, no. 3 (November/December 1976).

Jette, Alan M., Sharon L. Tennstedt, and Laurence G. Branch. "Stability of Informal Long-Term Care." *Journal of Housing for the Elderly*, 4, no. 2 (May 1992): 193-211.

Katz, Alfred H. Self-Help Organizations and Volunteer Participation in Social Welfare." *Social Work*, no. 15 (January 1970): 51-60.

Katz, Alfred H., and Eugene I. Bender. *The Strength in Us: Self-Help Groups in the Modern World*. New York: New Viewpoint, a Division of Franklin Watts, 1976.

Kaye, Lenard W., and Abraham Monk. "Social Relations in Enriching Housing for the Aged: A Case Study." *Journal of Housing for the Elderly*, 9, nos. 1-2 (1991): 111-126.

Kerschner, Paul A., ed. *Advocacy and Age: Issues, Experiences, Strategies*. Los Angeles, CA: Ethel Percy Andrus Gerontology Center, University of Southern California, 1976.

Knopf, Olga. *Successful Aging*. New York: The Viking Press, 1975.

Kornblum, Seymour. "The Meaning of a Volunteer Role to the Aged." *Readers Digest*, Spring 1979.

Lieberman, Morton H., Leonard D. Borman, and Associates. *Self-Help Groups for Coping with Crisis*. San Francisco: Jossey-Bass Publishers, 1979.

Litwak, Eugene. *Helping the Elderly: The Complementary Roles of Informal Networks and Formal Systems*. New York: Guilford Press.

Litwak, Eugene, in collaboration with John Dono, Cecilia Falbe, Barbara Kail, Steve Kulis, Sam Marillo, and Roger Sherman. "The Modified Extended Family, Social Networks, and Research Continuities in Aging." Monograph prepared for a University Seminar, Duke University, Durham, N.C., June 1981. (Research supported by grants from National Institute on Aging, no. R01AG00654 and the National Institute for Mental Health no. R01MH30726.)

Litwak, Eugene, and Steve Kulis. "The Dynamics of Network Change for Older People: Social Policy and Social Theory." Monograph, June 1981, Columbia University Center for the Social Sciences and the School of Social Work. (Research supported by grant from the National Institute on Aging and the National Institute of Mental Health, Grant no. ROLAG00564 and ROIM30726.)

Litwak, Eugene, and Margaret J. Shepherd. "Parents as Co-Teachers of Learning Disabled Children: A Test of the Theory of Coordination of Primary Groups and Formal Organizations." Proposal submitted for grants under handicapped research and demonstration programs, Columbia University, January 10, 1977.

Lopata, Helena Znaniecki. "Social Relations of Widows in Black and White Urban Communities." Social and Family Relations of Black Widows in Urban Communities. U.S. Department of Health, Education, and Welfare, Social and Rehabilitation Services, Administration on Aging, unpublished research.

Lopata, Helena Znaniecki. "Support Systems of Elderly Urbanites: Chicago in the 1970s." *The Gerontologist*, 15, no. 1 (1975): 35-41.

Mayer, Mary J. "Kin and Neighbors: Differential Roles in Differing Cultures." Paper presented at 29th Annual Gerontological Society Meeting, New York, October 1976.

McKinlay, John B. "Social Networks, Lay Consultation and Help-Seeking Behavior." *Social Forces*, 51 (March 1973): 275-292.

Mellor, M. Joanna, Harriet Rzetelny, and Iris E. Hudis. "Self-Help Groups for Caregivers of the Aged." Paper presented at First Annual Symposium: Social Work with Groups, Cleveland, Ohio, December 1979. [Research supported by grant no. 90-A-1609 (01) from the Model Projects on Aging Program, Administration on Aging.]

Monk, Abraham. "Family Supports in Old Age." *Social Work*, 24, no. 6 (November 1979): 533-538.

Monk, Abraham, ed. *The Age of Aging, a Reader in Social Gerontology*. Buffalo, N.Y.: Prometheus Books, 1979.

National Association of Social Workers. *Encyclopedia of Social Work*. Sixteenth issue, Vol. II, 1973.

New York State Office for the Aging. *Family Caregiving and the Elderly: Policy Recommendations and Research Findings*. Monograph, March 1983.

The 1980 Census of Population and Housing (Supplementary Report). PHC80-S1-1. Department of Commerce, Bureau of Census, March 1982.

Polansky, Norman A., ed. *Social Work Research*. Chicago: The University of Chicago Press, 1960.

Popham, W. James, and Kenneth A. Sirotnik. *Educational Statistics: Use and Interpretation*. New York: Harper & Row Publishers, 1973.

Pressman, Hope Hughes. *A New Resource for Welfare Reform: The Poor Themselves*. Berkeley: Institute of Governmental Studies, University of California, 1975.

Seguin, Mary M. "Opportunity for Peer Socialization in a Retirement Community." *The Gerontologist*, Summer 1973, 208-218.

Selltiz, Clair, Lawrence S. Wrightsman, and Stuart W. Cook. *Research Methods in Social Relations*. New York: Holt, Rinehart and Winston, 1976.

Shapiro, Joan Hatch. *Communities of the Alone*. New York: Association Press, 1971.

Sherman, Susan R. "Mutual Assistance and Support in Retirement Housing." *Journal of Gerontology*, 30, no. 4 (1975): 479-483.

Sherman, Susan R. "Patterns of Contacts for Residents of Age-Segregated and Age-Integrated Housing." *Journal of Gerontology*, 30, no. 1 (1975): 103-107.

Sidel, Victor W., and Ruth Sidel. "Beyond Coping." *Social Policy*, September/October 1976, 67-69.

Silverman, Phyllis R. "Mutual Help Groups." *Encyclopedia of Social Work*. 18th edition, 171-176. National Association of Social Work, 1984.

Silverman, Phyllis R. "Transitions and Models of Intervention." In *The Annals of the American Academy of Political and Social Science* (Special Issue), ed. F. Berado, 174-187.

Taeuber, Cynthia M. *Sixty-Five Plus in America*. Current Population Reports, Special Studies. U.S. Department of Commerce, Economics and Statistics Administration, Bureau of the Census, 1992.

Taylor, Robert Joseph. "Receipt of Support from Family Among Black Americans: Demographic and Familial Differences." *Journal of Marriage and the Family*, no. 48 (February 1986): 67-77.

Traunstein, Donald M., and Richard Steinman. "Voluntary Self-Help Organizations: An Exploratory Study" *Journal of Voluntary Action Research*, no. 4 (1973): 230-239.

Wentowski, Gloria J. "Reciprocity and the Coping Strategies of Older People: Cultural Dimensions of Network Building." *The Gerontologist*, 21, no. 6 (1981): 600-609.

APPENDIX A
SELF-HELP GROUPS INTERVIEW GUIDE

NAME...

ADDRESS...

1. Length of time in: (IF LESS THAN ONE YEAR, CODE AS 99;
   WRITE NUMBER OF YEARS IN THE BLANK SPACE)
   (A) Group.................years
   (B) Neighborhood..........years
   (C) Building..............years

(FOR QUESTIONS 2-6 CIRCLE THE NUMBER BEFORE THE
CORRECT ANSWER)
2. What was your age on your last birthday?
   1. 60-65
   2. 66-70
   3. 71-75
   4. 76-80
   5. 81-85
   6. 86-above
   0. No response/don't know

3. Sex of respondent:
   1. Male
   2. Female

4. What is the origin of birth?
   1. Irish
   2. Italian
   3. WASP
   4. Black (Negro)
   5. Oriental
   6. German Jewish
   7. Russian Jewish
   8. Hispanic

117

9.   Other
0.   No response/don't know

5.   Where did you spend the major portion of your childhood years?
     (WRITE IN THE NAME OF THE STATE IN THE SPACE
     PROVIDED)
     1.   Northeast
     2.   North Central
     3.   South
     4.   West
     5.   Outside Continental United States
     0.   No response/don't know

6.   What is your marital status?
     1.   Single (never married)
     2.   Married
     3.   Widow/widower
     4.   Divorced
     5.   Separated
     6.   Other
     0.   No response/don't know

7.   Socioeconomic status: (WRITE ANSWER IN BLANK SPACE)
     Subject's occupation a)......................
     Previous occupation b)......................
     Spouse's occupation c)......................
     Spouse's previous occupation d)..............

8.   Education: How far did you go in school?

     8a. *Subject*
     1.   0-4 years
     2.   5-8 years
     3.   High school incomplete
     4.   High school completed
     5.   Post-high school (business/trade school)
     6.   1-3 years of college
     7.   4 years of college
     8.   Post-graduate school

8b. *Spouse*
1.   0-4 years
2.   5-8 years
3.   High school incomplete
4.   High school completed
5.   Post-high school (business/trade school)
6.   1-3 years of college
7.   4 years of college
8.   Post-graduate school

8c. Income in last major/full-time job
1.   Under $1,500
2. $ 1,500-$ 2,499
3. $ 2,500-$ 3,999
4. $ 4,000-$ 5,999
5. $ 6,000-$ 7,999
6. $ 8,000-$ 9,999
7. $10,000-$12,999
8. $13,000-$15,999
9. $16,000-over

9.   a.   Please tell me if you ever go to any of the following places (GO THROUGH LIST BELOW) (GO TO FIRST PLACE CHECKED *YES* IN Q9a AND ASK Q9b-f. THEN PROCEED TO OTHER PLACES CHECKED YES IN Q9a AND CONTINUE ASKING Q9b-f FOR EACH PLACE IN TURN)

Code:
1 = grocery store
2 = butcher
3 = drugstore
4 = doctor/clinic
5 = clothing store
6 = church/synagogue

	1	2	3	4	5	6

9a. Ever go......
1. Yes

	1	1	1	1	1	1
2. No

| | 2 | 2 | 2 | 2 | 2 | 2 |
3. Don't know

| | 3 | 3 | 3 | 3 | 3 | 3 |

9b. Where......
1. Inside neighborhood

| 1 | 1 | 1 | 1 | 1 | 1 |
2. Outside neighborhood

| 2 | 2 | 2 | 2 | 2 | 2 |

9c. Distance (blocks)
1. 1- 3

| 1 | 1 | 1 | 1 | 1 | 1 |
2. 4- 6

| 2 | 2 | 2 | 2 | 2 | 2 |
3. 7-10

| 3 | 3 | 3 | 3 | 3 | 3 |
4. 11-20

| 4 | 4 | 4 | 4 | 4 | 4 |
5. 21-more

| 5 | 5 | 5 | 5 | 5 | 5 |

9d. Frequency......
1. Daily

| 1 | 1 | 1 | 1 | 1 | 1 |
2. More than once a week

| 2 | 2 | 2 | 2 | 2 | 2 |
3. Once a week

| 3 | 3 | 3 | 3 | 3 | 3 |
4. 2-3 times a month

| 4 | 4 | 4 | 4 | 4 | 4 |
5. Once a month

| 5 | 5 | 5 | 5 | 5 | 5 |
6. Several times a year

| 6 | 6 | 6 | 6 | 6 | 6 |
7. Once a year or less

| 7 | 7 | 7 | 7 | 7 | 7 |

9e. Mode of travel......
1. Walk

| 1 | 1 | 1 | 1 | 1 | 1 |
2. Bus

| 2 | 2 | 2 | 2 | 2 | 2 |
3. Subway

| 3 | 3 | 3 | 3 | 3 | 3 |
4. Car

| 4 | 4 | 4 | 4 | 4 | 4 |
5. Other

| 5 | 5 | 5 | 5 | 5 | 5 |

9f. Specify: .. ..

Code:

7 = bank
8 = park
9 = movie/theatre
10 = club/organization
11 = job/business
12 = bar or restaurant

		7	8	9	10	11	12
9a. Ever go......							
	1. Yes	1	1	1	1	1	1
	2. No	2	2	2	2	2	2
	3. Don't know	3	3	3	3	3	3
9b. Where......							
	1. Inside neighborhood	1	1	1	1	1	1
	2. Outside neighborhood	2	2	2	2	2	2
9c. Distance (blocks)							
	1. 1- 3	1	1	1	1	1	1
	2. 4- 6	2	2	2	2	2	2
	3. 7-10	3	3	3	3	3	3
	4. 11-20	4	4	4	4	4	4
	5. 21-more	5	5	5	5	5	5
9d. Frequency.....							
	1. Daily	1	1	1	1	1	1
	2. More than once a week	2	2	2	2	2	2
	3. Once a week	3	3	3	3	3	3
	4. 2-3 times a month	4	4	4	4	4	4
	5. Once a month	5	5	5	5	5	5
	6. Several times a year	6	6	6	6	6	6
	7. Once a year or less	7	7	7	7	7	7

9e. Mode of travel......
    1. Walk   1 1 1   1   1   1
    2. Bus   2 2 2   2   2   2
    3. Subway   3 3 3   3   3   3
    4. Car   4 4 4   4   4   4
    5. Other   5 5 5   5   5   5

9f. Specify   .. ..
                                    .. ..

10. With whom do you go to the following places? WRITE THE NUMBER OF THE CORRECT ANSWER IN THE BLANK SPACE)
Code:
1. Alone
2. Family
3. Friend
4. Neighbor
5. Group member (social/activity)
6. Other (specify in space probided)
0. No response/does not apply

    a. Grocery store................................
    b. Butcher......................................
    c. Drugstore....................................
    d. Doctor/clinic................................
    e. Clothing store...............................
    f. Church/synagogue.............................
    g. Bank...
    h. Park...
    i. Movie/theatre................................
    j. Club/organization............................
    k. Bar/restaurant...............................

11. a. Are you a member of a resident/social/activity group in this development/center?
        1. Yes
        2. No (IF THE ANSWER IS NO GO TO Q.22.c)

11. b. How often do you attend?
    1. Very often
    2. Fairly often
    3. Only occasionally
    0. No response

11. c. Are you a member of a group outside this development/center?
    1. Yes
    2. No (IF THE ANSWER TO THE QUESTION IS NO PROCEED TO Q.12)

11. d. How often do you attend?
    1. Very often
    2. Fairly often
    3. Only occasionally
    0. No response

12. Would you say that the members of the groups you belong to do the following things for each other; if so, how often? (CIRCLE THE NUMBER UNDER THE CORRECT ANSWER FOR EACH ITEM)

Code:
1 = not at all
2 = very often
3 = fairly often
4 = only occasionally

		1	2	3	4
1.	Visit with each other	1	2	3	4
2.	Help you when you are ill	1	2	3	4
3.	Give you advice on money matters	1	2	3	4
4.	Help you make a decision on a big purchase	1	2	3	4
5.	Shop or run errands for you	1	2	3	4
6.	Give you gifts	1	2	3	4
7.	Help fix things around the house	1	2	3	4
8.	Provide conversation	1	2	3	4
9.	Help with minor household tasks	1	2	3	4
10.	Help prepare meals for you, but not keep house	1	2	3	4
11.	Go on trips together	1	2	3	4
12.	Help you out with money	1	2	3	4

13.   Provide moral support in
      time of crisis   1   2   3   4

13.   Most people join groups for different reasons. I am now going to
      read off some items, and I want you to tell me in the order of
      importance to you the three (3) most important reasons for your
      joining the groups.   (RANK IN THE ORDER OF
      IMPORTANCE. LIST ONLY THREE CHOICES.)
      0.   No response   *Code*
      1.   Get help from others   1st choice...............
      2.   Give help to others   2nd choice..............
      3.   Meet friends   3rd choice..............
      4.   Help friends
      5.   Because I could not get help from a social service agency
      6.   To gain power for senior citizens
      7.   Because I was a member when I was younger
      8.   We have similar needs and can help each other
      9.   Similar groups were helpful to me

14.   During the past year, have you been to a social service agency?
      1.   Yes
      2.   No (IF THE ANSWER TO THE QUESTION IS NO, SKIP
           TO Q.16)
      0.   No response

15.   People have different experiences with social service agencies that
      are meant to serve them; which of the following statements comes
      closest to your experience with social service agencies. (CIRCLE
      THE NUMBER IN FRONT OF THE CORRECT RESPONSE.)

      a.   The interview and paper work at the social service agency was
           time consuming and confusing.
           1. Yes 2. No 0. No response/does not apply
      b.   The staff was not friendly and helpful.
           1. Yes 2. No 0. No response/does not apply
      c.   The staff was able to help me with my needs/problems.
           1. Yes 2. No 0. No response/does not apply
      d.   The staff was friendly and patient but not helpful.
           1. Yes 2. No 0. No response/does not apply

e. I feel that the social service agency will not help me if I ask for help.
   1. Yes 2. No 0. No response/does not apply
f. Why?..
....
....

16. From time to time, all of us are faced with situations where we might need help. I will read some of these situations to you; for each one, please tell me who, if anyone, you would be most likely to turn to if you were in that situation. Let's start with an instance where (READ THE FIRST SITUATION)--who, if anyone, would you turn to or call? (CONTINUE THROUGH LIST. IF RESPONDENT SAYS WIFE/HUSBAND, ASK) Suppose your wife/husband were not available; who would you turn to?

Code:
0. No response/does not apply/don't know
1. No one
2. Myself
3. Child
4. Other relatives
5. Friend
6. Neighbor
7. Social agency
8. Social/activity group
   9. Other   SPECIFY IF OTHER
                               WAS INDICATED

a. You suddenly feel sick   a1................
   or dizzy

b. You want to talk to   b1................
   someone   about   a
   problem   concerning
   your child or someone
   else in your family

c. You need to borrow a   c1................
   few dollars until your
   next check comes

d. You feel lonely and   d1................
    want to talk

e. You need a new light   e1................
    bulb in the ceiling

f. You need someone to   f1................
    help you get to the
    doctor

g. You find you do not   g1................
    have enough money to
    cover a very big
    medical bill

h. You are in the hospital   h1................
    and need someone to
    look after your
    apartment

i. You need someone to   i1................
    help you fill out a
    form

j. You have an accident   j1................
    and need someone to
    come in each day to
    bathe and help you
    take your medicine

17. a. As you probably know, there are special groups of agencies in New York City which help older people with any difficulties they might have. During the *past year*, have you turned to any of the following?

(GO THROUGH LIST: FOR EACH AGENCY OR GROUP CHECKED "YES" IN Q17.a. ASK Q.17.b.

b. Did you get the help you needed? (IF NO, ASK) Why not? What happened? (17.c)

Q.17.a.

		N/R	Agencies Turned to Yes	No
1.	Social Security Office	0	1	2
2.	The Office for the Aging	0	1	2
3.	Department of Social Services	0	1	2
4.	Police	0	1	2
5.	New York City Housing Authority (public housing)	0	1	2
6.	Senior Center	0	1	2
7.	Settlement House	0	1	2
8.	Visiting Nurse Service	0	1	2
9.	Home Health Aide or Homemaker Service	0	1	2
10.	Family Service Agency	0	1	2
11.	Employment Agency	0	1	2
12.	Nursing home or Home for the Aged	0	1	2
13.	Minister, Priest, Rabbi	0	1	2
14.	Spiritualist	0	1	2
15.	Other agency: .... (specify)	0	1	2

Q17.b   Help
                                                          Received
                                                    N/R   Yes   No

		N/R	Yes	No
1.	Social Security Office	0	1	2
2.	The Office for the Aging	0	1	2
3.	Department of Social Services	0	1	2
4.	Police	0	1	2
5.	New York City Housing Authority (public housing)	0	1	2
6.	Senior Center	0	1	2
7.	Settlement House	0	1	2
8.	Visiting Nurse Service	0	1	2
9.	Home Health Aide or Homemaker Service	0	1	2
10.	Family Service Agency	0	1	2
11.	Employment Agency	0	1	2
12.	Nursing Home or Home for the Aged	0	1	2
13.	Minister, Priest, Rabbi	0	1	2
14.	Spiritualist	0	1	2
15.	Other agency: .... (specify)	0	1	2

Q.17.c   Reasons for Not
                                                    Receiving Help

1.	Social Security Office	....
2.	The Office for the Aging	....
3.	Department of Social Services	....
4.	Police	....
5.	New York City Housing Authority (public housing)	....
6.	Senior Center	....
7.	Settlement House	....
8.	Visiting Nurse Service	....
9.	Home Health Aide or Homemaker service	....
10.	Family Service Agency	....
11.	Employment Agency	....
12.	Nursing Home or Home for the Aged	....
13.	Minister, Priest, Rabbi	....

14. Spiritualist   ....

15. Other agency:

      ....

          (specify)

18. a. Now I would like to know a few things about your family. How many children, if any, have you *had* or *adopted in all*? (IF HAVE *HAD* OR *ADOPTED* CHILDREN, ASK q.18.b-c. IF *NONE* SKIP TO q.18.C.)

  b. How many are presently living?

  c. How many other children, if any, have you raised or been solely responsible for?

    Code:

    Q.18.a: Children have had or adopted

    Q.18.b: Children living

    Q.18.c: Other children raised

	Q.18.a	Q.18.b	Q.18.c
1 child	1	1	1
2 children	2	2	2
3 children	3	3	3
4-5 children	4	4	4
6-7 children	5	5	5
8-10 children	6	6	6
11 or more children	7	7	7
no response/does not apply	0	0	0

(IF RESPONDENT HAS *LIVING CHILDREN*, OR HAS *RAISED OTHER CHILDREN*, ASK Q.19.a: OTHERS, SKIP TO Q.26.)

19. a. Please give me the first names of all your living children. (IF
       OTHER CHILDREN RAISED [REFER TO Q.18c], ASK:
       Now give me the first names of other children you may have
       raised who are still living. [LIST THE NAMES BELOW--
       USE NEXT PAGE IF NECESSARY]).
       (FOR FIRST CHILD LISTED IN Q.19.a, ASK Q.19.b-g;
       THEN ASK Q.19.b-g, IN TURN FOR EACH OF THE
       OTHER CHILDREN LISTED)
    b. Is (NAME) a male or female?
    c. How old is he/she?
    d. Where does (NAME) live? (PROBE FOR CATEGORIES
       LISTED BELOW--WITH RESPONDENT.   IN SAME
       BUILDING, WITHIN WALKING DISTANCE, ETC.)
    e. About how often do you see him/her?
    f. About how often do you talk with him/her on the phone?
    g. Would you say that the two of you are *very close, fairly close,
       not too close*, or *not close at all?*

		NAMES OF CHILDREN			
		1)....2)....3)....4)....			
b.	Sex	19b.1	19b.2	19b.3	19b.4
	Male	1	1	1	1
	Female	2	2	2	2
c.	Age	19c.1	19c.2	19c.3	19c.4
	Under 18 years	1	1	1	1
	18-24 years	2	2	2	2
	25-34 years	3	3	3	3
	35-44 years	4	4	4	4
	45-54 years	5	5	5	5
	55 years or over	6	6	6	6
d.	Where lives	19d.1	19d.2	19d.3	19d.4
	With respondent	1	1	1	1
	Same building as respondent	2	2	2	2
	Within walking distance	3	3	3	3
	Within city limits	4	4	4	4

		19...1	19...2	19...3	19...4
	In same metropolitan area	5	5	5	5
	Beyond metropolitan area	6	6	6	6
e.	Frequency of seeing	19e.1	19e.2	19e.3	19e.4
	Every day	1	1	1	1
	Every week	2	2	2	2
	Every month	3	3	3	3
	Several times a year	4	4	4	4
	Once a year or less	5	5	5	5
f.	Frequency of talking on phone	19f.1	19f.2	19f.3	19f.4
	Every day	1	1	1	1
	Every week	2	2	2	2
	Every month	3	3	3	3
	Several times a year	4	4	4	4
	Once a year or less	5	5	5	5
g.	Closeness	19g.1	19g.2	19g.3	19g.4
	Very close	1	1	1	1
	Fairly close	2	2	2	2
	Not too close	3	3	3	3
	Not close at all	4	4	4	4
	No response	0	0	0	0

NAMES OF CHILDREN
5)...6)...7)...8)...

		19b.1	19b.2	19b.3	19b.4
b.	Sex	19b.1	19b.2	19b.3	19b.4
	Male	1	1	1	1
	Female	2	2	2	2
c.	Age	19c.1	19c.2	19c.3	19c.4
	Under 18 years	1	1	1	1
	18-24 years	2	2	2	2
	25-34 years	3	3	3	3
	35-44 years	4	4	4	4
	45-54 years	5	5	5	5
	55 years or over	6	6	6	6

D. Where lives	19d.1	19d.2	19d.3	19d.4
With respondent	1	1	1	1
Same building as respondent	2	2	2	2
Within walking distance	3	3	3	3
Within city limits	4	4	4	4
In the same metropolitan area	5	5	5	5
Beyond metropolitan area	6	6	6	6

e. Frequency of seeing	19e.1	19e.2	19e.3	19e.4
Every day	1	1	1	1
Every week	2	2	2	2
Every month	3	3	3	3
Several times a year	4	4	4	4
Once a year or less	5	5	5	5

f. Frequency of talking on phone	19f.1	19f.2	19f.3	19f.4
Every day	1	1	1	1
Every week	2	2	2	2
Every month	3	3	3	3
Several times a year	4	4	4	4
Once a year or less	5	5	5	5

g. Closeness	19g.1	19g.2	19g.3	19g.4
Very close	1	1	1	1
Fairly close	2	2	2	2
Not too close	3	3	3	3
Not close at all	4	4	4	4
No response	0	0	0	0

19. h. Would you like to see your child/children more often, about the same, or less often than you do now?
More often = 1...ASK q.19i
About the same = 2...SKIP TO Q20.a.
Less often = 3...
No response = 0...

i. What are the things that keep you from getting together more often? Anything else?

....
....
....

20. a. As you know, parents and children sometimes help each other in different ways? Do you ever help your child/children in any of the following ways? (GO THROUGH LIST: FOR EACH ITEM CHECKED YES IN Q.20a ASK 20b.)

b. On the average, do you do this very often, fairly often, occasionally?

Q.20.a

			Ever help	
		N/R	Yes	No
1.	Help out when someone is ill	0	1	2
2.	Babysit for a while when parents are out	0	1	2
3.	Give advice on running a home and bringing up your grandchildren	0	1	2
4.	Shop or run errands	0	1	2
5.	Give gifts	0	1	2
6.	Help your child/children out with money	0	1	2
7.	Fix things around their/his/her house	0	1	2
8.	Give advice on jobs and business matters	0	1	2
9.	Help them/hi /her make a decision on a big purchase, such as a car	0	1	2
10.	Keep house for them/him/her	0	1	2

Q.20.b   Frequency

Code: 1 = very often   1   2   3   0
       2 = fairly often
       3 = only occasionally
       0 = N/R

1. Help out when someone is ill   1   2   3   0
2. Babysit for a while when parents
    are out   1   2   3   0
3. Give advice on running a home
    and bringing up your grandchildren   1   2   3   0
4. Shop or run errands   1   2   3   0
5. Give gifts   1   2   3   0
6. Help your child/children out
    with money   1   2   3   0
7. Fix things around their/his/her
    house   1   2   3   0
8. Give advice on jobs and business
    matters   1   2   3   0
9. Help them/him/her make a decision
    on a big purchase, such as a car   1   2   3   0
10. Keep house for them/him/her   1   2   3   0

21. a. Now, I would like to know if your child/children ever
       helps/help you in any of the following ways. (GO THROUGH
       LIST.) (FOR EACH ITEM CHECKED YES IN Q.21.a ASK
       Q.21b.)
    b. On the average, does he/she (do they) do this very often,
       fairly often, or only occasionally?

Q.21.a   Ever help
                                             N/R   Yes   No

1. Help you when you are ill (or
    when your wife/husband is ill)   0   1   2
2. Give you advice on money matters   0   1   2
3. Help you make a decision on a
    big purchase   0   1   2
4. Shop or run errands for you   0   1   2
5. Give you gifts   0   1   2
6. Help fix things around the house   0   1   2
7. Keep house for you   0   1   2

8.	Prepare meals for you, but not keep house	0	1	2
9.	Take you away during the summer	0	1	2
10.	Help you out with money	0	1	2
11.	Drive you places, such as the doctor, shopping, church	0	1	2

Q.21.b

Code: 1 = very often
        2 = fairly often
        3 = only occasionally
        0 = N/R

		Frequency			
		1	2	3	0
1.	Help you when you are ill (or when your wife/husband is ill)	1	2	3	0
2.	Give you advice on money matters	1	2	3	0
3.	Help you make a decision on a big purchase	1	2	3	0
4.	Shop or run errands for you	1	2	3	0
5.	Give you gifts	1	2	3	0
6.	Help fix things around the house	1	2	3	0
7.	Keep house for you	1	2	3	0
8.	Prepare meals for you, but not keep house	1	2	3	0
9.	Take you away during the summer	1	2	3	0
10.	Help you out with money	1	2	3	0
11.	Drive you places, such as the doctor, shopping, church	1	2	3	0

22. a. How many grandchildren, if any, do you have? (IF HAS GRANDCHILDREN, ASK Q22.b; OTHERS, SKIP TO Q.26.)

   b. And how many great grandchildren, if any, do you have?

	Q.22.a No. of grand- children	Q.22.b No. of great grand- children
None	1	1
1- 2	2	2
3- 4	3	3
5- 7	4	4
8-12	5	5
13-16	6	6
17 or more	7	7

23. Do you ever take care of your grandchildren or great grandchildren while their parents work?
1....Yes (ASK Q.24.a)
2....No (SKIP TO Q.26)

24. a. Do you do this every week or just once in a while?
1....every week (ASK Q.24b)
2....once in a while (SKIP TO Q.25.a)

24. b. About how many hours a week do you spend taking care of them, on the average?
1.... 1- 5
2.... 6-10
3....11-20
4....21-40
5....41 hours or more

25. a. How do you feel about taking care of your grandchildren or
       great grandchildren? Would you say that this is something
       you prefer to do, or do you wish you had more time to do
       other things?
       1....prefer taking care of grandchildren (SKIP TO Q.26a)
       2....would like to do other things (ASK q.25b)

    b. Why do you feel this way? Anything else?
       ....
       ....

26. a. Do you have any living brothers or sisters?
       1....Yes (ASK Q.26.b)
       2....No (SKIP TO Q.29a)

    b. How many in all?
       1.................
       2.................
       3.................
       4.................
       5.................
       6 or more..........

27. a. How many of your brothers and sisters, if any, live in the
       building?
    b. How many, if any, live within walking distance from here?
    c. And how many, if any, live in New York City?

	Q27a In the Building	Q27b Within Walking Distance	Q27c In New York City
None	1	1	1
1	2	2	2
2	3	3	3
3	4	4	4
4	5	5	5
5	6	6	6
6 or more	7	7	7

28. a. How often do you see a brother or sister?
    b. And how often do you talk to a brother or sister on the phone?

	Q.28.a See	Q.28.b Talk to on Phone
Every day	1	1
Every week	2	2
Every month	3	3
Several times a year	4	4
Once a year or less	5	5

29. a. Do any of your relatives, other than children or brothers and sisters, live in this building?
       (IF YES TO Q.29a ASK Q.29b-c.   OTHERS SKIP TO Q.30.a)
    b. How many?
    c. What relation are they to you?

30. a. Do any of your relatives, other than children or brothers and sisters, live within walking distance from here?
       (IF YES TO Q.30.a ASK Q.30.b-c.   OTHERS SKIP TO Q.31.)

	29 Relatives in Building	30 Relatives Within Walking Distance
a. Have them		
Yes	1	1
No	2	2
b. How many		
1	1	1
2	2	2
3	3	3
4	4	4
5 or more	5	5

c.   Relation

Father	1	1
Mother	2	2
Aunt	3	3
Uncle	4	4
Cousin	5	5
Other	6	6

31.   Think of all the relatives you have in New York City, other than children or brothers and sisters. How many do you see or hear from regularly?

0...............No Response
1...............1
2...............2
3...............3
4...............4
5 or more....5

32.   a.   Please tell me if you belong to any of the following groups of organizations. (GO THROUGH LIST BELOW.) Any others that I didn't name? (LIST BELOW)
      b.   Is (CLUB OR ORGANIZATION) for older people only?

		Q.32.a			Q.32.b Older People Only	
			Belong			
		N/R	Yes	No	Yes	No
1.	A group of close friends who meet together, visit each other, and do things for each other	0	1	2	1	2
2.	A labor union	0	1	2	1	2
3.	A church or synagogue group	0	1	2	1	2
4.	A Senior Center or Golden Age Club	0	1	2	1	2
5.	A family circle or club made up of people from your home town	0	1	2	1	2

6.	Other...............................	1	2
7.	Other...............................	1	2

32. c. Would you say you go there frequently, occasionally, or
   rarely?

   Code: Frequency
   1 = frequently   1 2 3 0
   2 = occasionally
   3 = rarely
   0 = N/R

1.	A group of close friends who meet together, visit each other, and do things for each other	1	2	3	0
2.	A labor union	1	2	3	0
3.	A church or synagogue group	1	2	3	0
4.	A Senior Center or Golden Age Club	1	2	3	0
5.	A family circle or club made up of people from your home town	1	2	3	0
6.	Other...	1	2	3	0
7.	Other...	1	2	3	0

32. d. Were you a member of similar groups during your earlier
   life?
   Yes.....................1 (ASK Q.32.e)
   No......................2 (SKIP TO 33)
   N/R.....................0

32. e. Earlier in life would you say that you visited these groups
   frequently, occasionally, or only rarely?
   Frequently.....................1
   Occasionally...................2
   Rarely.........................3
   N/R............................0

33. We would like to know something about the groups you belong
   to:

			33a		
a.	To how many social/friendship/ activity groups do you belong?	1-2	3-5	6 or more	none
		1	2	3	0

		33b	
	3-4	5-10	11 or more	don't know

b. On the average about how many members are in these groups?

	3-4	5-10	11 or more	don't know
	1	2	3	0

c. These social/friendship activity groups include

33c

	Yes	No	Don't Know	No Response
1. Men only	1	2	3	0
2. Women only	1	2	3	0
3. Both men and women	1	2	3	0
4. Neighbors only	1	2	3	0
5. Friends only	1	2	3	0
6. Friends and neighbors	1	2	3	0
7. People from the neighborhood only	1	2	3	0
8. People from my building only	1	2	3	0
9. People from this housing development only	1	2	3	0
10. People from this borough only	1	2	3	0
11. Older people only	1	2	3	0
12. People from all over New York City	1	2	3	0

33. d. How many activities do you participate in each week on an average?

34. We would like to know about the group's relationship to Social Service or professional agencies: To which of the following categories do your group belong?

	Yes	No	Don't Know	No Response
a. Is connected to a social service agency	1	2	3	0
b. Is supervised by a professional person (paid staff)	1	2	3	0
c. Get advice from a professional				

person (paid staff)	1	2	3	0
d. Get economic support from a professional group/agency	1	2	3	0
e. Do not get help from a professional agency/group	1	2	3	0
f. Could be more helpful if it was connected to a professional agency	1	2	3	0

g. Why...............................
....

h. Would be less helpful if it was connected to a professional agency	1	2	3	0

i. Why?...............................
....

35. a. Some people say that if older people organize as a group, they would have the power to get the things older people need. Do you agree or disagree with this?

        Agree.........................1 (ASK Q.35b)
        Disagree......................2
        Don't know....................3 (SKIP TO Q.36a)
        No response...................0

    b. Why do you feel this way? Anything else?

....
....
....

36. a. Have you ever taken any action on behalf of older people-- such as going to meetings, writing letters, demonstrating and so forth?

        Yes......................1 (ASK Q.36b)
        No......................2 (SKIP TO Q.37)
        N/R......................0

    b. What did you do? Anything else?

....
....
....

37. Did you vote in the recent national election?

        Yes........................1
        No.........................2
        N/R.......................3

Thank you very much for all your time and assistance. I've asked all the questions I need to ask. Are there any questions you would like to ask me? Are there any comments or suggestions you wish to make?

APPENDIX B
MEMORANDUM

ASSOCIATED YM-YWHAs OF GREATER NEW YORK

From: Irwin Golden   Date: August 22, 1980

To: Hillary Weinstein
          Arlene Nichols

Subject: Ed Grupper

Bessie Wright, one of our Columbia University Doctoral students, is now prepared to list a questionnaire for her research dissertation on the phenomena of the self-help aged.

I would appreciate all the assistance that you can give her, by reaching the older population serviced by you.

Hillary Weinstein, Reuther Houses, 711 Seagirt Avenue, Far Rockaway, NY   212: 327-0951

Arlene Nichols, Gustave Hartman Y, 710 Hartman Lane, Far Rockaway, NY   212: 471-0200

Ed Grupper, Marble Hill Senior Citizens Center, 5365 Broadway, Bronx, NY   212: 562-8551

cc: S. Kaplansky

APPENDIX C
PROTECTION OF HUMAN SUBJECTS STATEMENT

A study is being conducted of Associated YM-YWHA of Greater New York Centers that sponsor or support *Self-Help Activities* among the elderly. You have been selected to answer our questions because you are a member of one of these centers.

STATEMENT OF PROTECTION OF HUMAN SUBJECTS

We would like to ask you a few questions about your experiences/involvement with the Center's programs. In addition, some questions will be asked about the ways in which you help and receive help from your families, friends, and neighbors. We want to assure you that all your replies will be anonymous and completely confidential. You are free to refuse to answer any question or to discontinue the interview at any point.

University regulations require us to ask you to sign a consent form to show that your participation is voluntary. Could you please sign the statement on this page. It will be filed separately from the rest of the interview.

I understand the nature of the interview I am about to give and consent to be interviewed.

Signed:.................

Date:.................

APPENDIX D
LETTER TO SUBJECTS FROM ACTIVITIES
CENTER DIRECTOR

January 20th, 1981

Dear:

A project sponsored by the Associated YM-YWHAs of Greater New York is interested in getting your views about the activities and programs you engage in at Roy Reuther Center.

The information we receive from you hopefully will help in planning future programs/activities for you and others.

We would like you to attend a meeting in the Community Room of the Roy Reuther Center so that we can give you more information about our Project and answer any questions you may have.

The meeting will be held on Tuesday, January 27th, 1981 at 10:00 A.M. Please attend.

We look forward to seeing you then.

Very truly yours,

....
Hillary Weinstein, Director

....
Hazel Wasser, Pres. of "Y"

APPENDIX E
LETTER REQUESTING APPROVAL

630 St. Nicholas Avenue
New York, New York 10030
November 12, 1980

Professor Marjorie Cantor
Gerontological Center
Fordham University
Lincoln Center
New York, New York 10023

Dear Professor Cantor:

I am a doctoral student at Columbia University School of Social Services and I am in the process of doing exploratory research on the topic, "The Role of Self-Help Programs in Service Delivery Among the Elderly," as a part of my doctoral requirements.

Dr. Barbara Jones Morrison has been serving as consultant to me in the development of the questionnaire for my study. She has suggested that your questionnaire, "Survey of Older People in New York City" is an excellent one which has had broad exposure and usage. I have reviewed the questionnaire and found that many of the questions would be very helpful to me in developing my questionnaire. I am, therefore, requesting your permission to use some questions from your questionnaire with proper documentation.

I have attempted to reach you several times at Fordham University by telephone but have been unsuccessful. Therefore, I would appreciate receiving your permission to use the questionnaire in writing.

Thank you very much for your consideration of this request.

Very truly yours,

Bessie Wright

APPENDIX F
PERCENTS OF SUBJECTS FOR DAILY LIFE ACTIVITIES:
WITH WHOM, DISTANCE, AND TRANSPORTATION
(N=48)

	Don't Go	Alone	With Whom			Group Member
			Family	Friend	Neighbor	
Grocery store	6	48	23	15	8	--
Butcher	42	25	15	10	8	--
Drugstore	15	54	15	13	2	--
Doctor/clinic	10	65	21	4	--	--
Clothing store	27	25	25	21	2	--
Church/synagogue	44	31	17	6	2	--
Bank	8	56	17	17	2	21
Movie/theatre	29	10	17	21	4	17
Club organization	20	44	2	13	--	--
Job/business	100	--	--	--	--	15
Bar/restaurant	35	8	13	27	2	

Appendix F (continued)

	Don't Go	Distance	
		10 Blocks or Less	11 Blocks or More
Grocery store	6	49	45
Butcher	42	10	48
Drugstore	16	38	46
Doctor/clinic	10	18	72
Clothing store	27	0	73
Church/synagogue	44	37	19
Bank	8	46	46
Park	79	9	12
Movie/theatre	29	13	58
Club/organization	20	63	17
Job/business	100	--	--
Bar/restaurant	35	15	50

Appendix F (continued)

	Don't Go	Walk	Transportation	
			Public	Private
Grocery store	6	56	20	18
Butcher	42	18	22	18
Drugstore	16	35	27	20
Doctor/clinic	10	16	46	28
Clothing store	27	--	43	20
Church/synagogue	44	42	10	4
Bank	8	40	40	12
Park	79	6	19	6
Movie/theatre	29	10	46	15
Club/organization	20	66	10	4
Job/business	100	--	--	--
Bar restaurant	35	13	34	18

APPENDIX G
ITEM-TOTAL CORRELATIONS FOR HELP RECEIVED FROM FRIENDS
(N=48)

Help Received from Friends Scale (Cronbach's Alpha=.74)	Mean	sd	Median	Range	Item-Total Correlation
Visit with each other	2.3	1.02	2.18	1-4	.62
Help you when you are ill	1.9	1.07	1.46	1-4	.53
Shop or run errands for you	1.3	1.65	1.12	1-4	.23
Provide conversation	3.0	0.85	3.02	1-4	.43
Help prepare meals for you but not keep house	1.0	0.15	1.01	1-2	.19
Go on trips together	2.1	0.91	2.05	1-4	.60
Provide moral support in time of crisis	1.7	0.90	1.46	1-4	.53
Scale item average	1.9	0.51	1.70	1-3	
Independent items					
Give you advice on money matters	1.1	0.32	1.00	1-3	
Help you make a decision on a big purchase	1.0	0.20	1.02	1-2	
Give you gifts	1.4	0.58	1.30	1-3	
Help fix things around the house	1.0	0.00	1.00	1	
Help with minor household tasks	1.0	0.00	1.00	1	
Help you out with money	1.0	0.00	1.00	1	

1=not at all; 2=only occasionally; 3=fairly often; 4=very often

                              Self-Help Among The Elderly

APPENDIX H
ITEM-TOTAL CORRELATIONS FOR HELP RECEIVED FROM CHILDREN
(N=48)

Help Received from Children Scale (Cronbach's Alpha = .85)	*Mean*	*sd*	*Median*	*Range*	*Item-Total Correlation*
Help you when you are ill (or when your spouse is ill)	1.8	0.90	1.50	1-4	.65
Give you advice on money matters	1.3	0.63	1.11	1-4	.57
Help you make a decision on a big purchase	1.3	0.62	1.12	1-4	.65
Shop or run errands for you	1.6	0.89	1.33	1-4	.83
Give you gifts	2.0	0.90	1.94	1-4	.68
Help fix things around the house	1.3	0.60	1.17	1-3	.32
Keep house for you	1.0	0.21	1.01	1-2	.28
Prepare meals for you but not keep house	1.1	0.25	1.03	1-2	.15
Take you away during the summer	1.2	0.51	1.07	1-3	.34
Drive you to places such as the doctor, shopping, etc.	1.5	0.79	1.21	1-4	.71
Scale item average	1.4	0.41	1.30	1-2.7	
Independent item: Help you out with money	1.0	0.00	1.0	1-2	

1 = not at all; 2 = only occasionally; 3 = fairly often; 4 = very often

APPENDIX I
ITEM-TOTAL CORRELATIONS FOR HELP GIVEN TO CHILDREN
(N=48)

Help Given to Children Scale (Cronbach's Alpha=.64)	Mean	sd	Median	Range	Item-Total Correlation
Help out when someone is ill	1.5	0.76	1.35	1-4	.55
Shop or run errands	1.1	0.25	1.05	1-3	.22
Give gifts	2.2	1.00	2.25	1-4	.41
Help your child/children out with money	1.3	0.64	1.17	1-4	.49
Fix things around their/his/her house	1.0	0.21	1.02	1-2	.53
Give advice on jobs and business matters	1.1	0.33	1.02	1-3	.21
Help them/him/her make a decision on a big purchase, such as a car	1.0	0.15	1.01	1-2	.43
Keep house for them/him/her	1.0	0.30	1.02	1-3	.37
Scale item average	1.3	0.30	1.30	1-2.3	
Independent items					
Babysit for a while when parents are out	1.0	0.26	1.00	1-2	
Give advice on running a home and bringing up grandchildren	1.0	0.21	1.00	1-2	

1=not at all; 2=only occasionally; 3=fairly often; 4=very often

APPENDIX J
FREQUENCIES FOR AGENCY-RELATED
ASSISTANCE ITEMS
(N=48)

	f	*%*
Question 16: Perception of Helping Sources		
a. You suddenly feel sick or dizzy	2	4
b. You want to talk to someone about a problem concerning your child or someone else in your family	7	15
c. You need to borrow a few dollars until your next check comes	2	4
d. You feel lonely and want to talk	2	4
e. You need a new light bulb in the ceiling	26	54
f. You need someone to help you get to the doctor	14	29
g. You find you do not have enough money to cover a very big medical bill	16	33
h. You are in the hospital and need someone to look after your apartment	2	4
i. You need someone to help you fill out a form	12	25
j. You have an accident and need someone to come in each day to bathe and help you take your medicine	25	52
Question 17: Agencies Turned to in Past Year		
1. Social Security Office	13	27
2. The Office for the Aging	0	--
3. Department of Social Services	6	13
4. Police	6	13
5. New York City Housing Authority (public housing)	7	15
6. Senior Center	16	33
7. Settlement House	0	--
8. Visiting Nurse Services	3	6
9. Home Health Aide or Homemaker Service	4	8
10. Family Service Agency	1	2
11. Employment Agency	1	2
12. Nursing Home or Home for the Aged	0	--
13. Minister, Priest, Rabbi	2	4
14. Spiritualist	0	--
15. Other Agency	0	--

APPENDIX K
SUMMARY STATISTICS FOR 14 INDEPENDENT
INTERVAL VARIABLES
(N=48)

	Mean	sd	Median	Range
Family Related				
Number of living children	1.50	1.29	1.56	0-6
Number of living children in				
metropolitan area	0.65	0.96	0.33	0-4
Number of living children				
seen monthly or more	0.70	0.46	0.98	0-4
Number of children with				
telephone contacts at				
least weekly	1.21	1.07	1.14	0-4
Number of siblings in				
metropolitan area	0.69	1.04	0.36	0-5
Mobility				
Ten blocks or less	2.96	1.95	2.79	0-7
More than ten blocks	4.79	2.60	4.93	0-9
On foot	2.98	1.97	2.83	0-7
Via public transportation	3.06	2.54	2.72	0-9
Via private transportation	1.67	2.58	0.42	0-9
Social Service Agencies				
Perception of formal agency as				
helping source	2.25	1.48	2.20	
Number of social agencies				
turned to for help	1.22	1.26	1.05	0-5
Number of non-senior social				
groups visited	1.96	0.97	1.81	1-4

APPENDIX L
SUMMARY STATISTICS FOR
SELF-HELP MEASURES
(N=48)

	Mean	*sd*	*Median*	*Range*
Number of Daily Life Activities				
Don't go	4.06	1.96	3.79	1-10
Go alone	3.71	2.59	3.36	0- 9
Go with family	1.82	2.77	0.35	0- 9
Go with friends	2.31	2.49	1.46	0-10
Help Received from Friends Scale	1.88	0.51	1.70	1- 3
Give you advice on money				
matters item	1.06	0.32	1.02	1- 3
Help you make a decision on				
a big purchase item	1.04	0.20	1.02	1- 2
Give you gifts item	1.42	0.58	1.30	1- 3
Help Given to Children Scale	1.30	0.30	1.25	1- 2.3
Babysit with grandchildren item	1.00	0.26	1.00	1- 2
Give advice on running a				
home and bringing up the				
bringing up the grand-				
children item	1.00	0.21	1.00	1- 2
Help Received from Children Scale	1.37	0.41	1.30	1- 2.7
Help you out with money item	1.00	0.00	1.00	1- 2
Perceptions of Helping Sources				
Turn to self	2.12	2.12	1.33	
Turn to relatives	2.65	2.47	2.00	
Turn to friends	2.98	2.35	2.83	

APPENDIX M
CORRELATIONS AMONG DIFFERENT SELF-HELP ACTIVITIES

Number of Daily Life Activities	1	2	3	4	5	6	7	8	9	10	11	12	13
1	--												
2	.07	--											
3	-.14	.50***	--										
4	-.41**	-.22	-.39**	--									
5	-.45***	-.22	-.11	.64**	--								
6	.29*	.05	-.02	-.18	-.17	--							
7	.10	.01	.17	.00	-.19	-.04	--						
8	.08	-.05	.17	.05	.00	.05	.04	--					
9	.04	-.17	.05	.09	.13	.00	.01	.24*	--				
10	.02	-.05	.17	.06	.09	-.03	-.03	.17	.00	--			
11	-.08	-.18	.05	-.03	.21	.12	-.01	.29*	.69***	-.08	--		

Appendix M (continued)
Number of Daily

Life Activities	1	2	3	4	5	6	7	8	9	10	11	12	13
12	.23	.06	.11	-.13	-.09	-.02	-.02	.11	.27*	.00	-.02	--	
13	.19	.10	.09	-.05	.02	-.05	-.05	.28*	-.02	.00	.07	-.02	--

1: Don't go; 2: Go alone; 3: Go with family; 4: Go with friends; 5: Help Received from Friends Scale; 6: Friend gives you advice on money matters; 7: Friend help you make a decision on a big purchase; 8: Friend give you gifts; 9: Help Received from Children Scale; 10: Children help you out with money; 11: Help given to children; 12: Elderly babysit with grandchildren; 13: Elderly give advice on running home and bringing up grandchildren

*p < .05   **p < .01   ***p < .001

APPENDIX N

CORRELATIONS BETWEEN THE ELDERLY'S PERCEPTION OF HELPING SOURCES: E.G., SELF, RELATIVES AND FRIENDS, AND 17 SELF-HELP MEASURES

(N=48)

	Elderly's Perception of Helping Sources			
	Turn to Self 1	Turn to Relatives 2	Turn to Friends 3	Group of Friends 4
Number of Daily Life Activities				
1. Don't go	-.24*	.08	-.01	-.34**
2. Go alone	-.10	-.19	.17	-.19
3. Go with family	.24*	.28*	-.36**	.08
4. Go with friends	.03	.01	.02	.28*
5. Help Received from Friends Scale	.07	.08	-.16	.30*
6. Friend give advice on money matters	-.06	-.08	-.01	-.11
7. Friend help with decision on big purchase	.11	.26*	.29*	-.11
8. Friend give you gifts	.13	.05	-.15	.14
9. Children Help Scale	.10	.23	-.22	.10
10. Children help out with money	-.07	.00	-.06	-.08

Appendix N (continued)

| | Elderly's Perception of Helping Sources | | | |
	Turn to Self 1	Turn to Relatives 2	Turn to Friends 3	Group of Friends 4
11. Help Given to Children Scale	.29*	.07	-.15	.18
12. Elderly babysit grandchildren	-.28*	.26*	-.15	-.25*
13. Elderly give advice on running home and bringing up grandchildren	-.21	-.02	.05	-.13**
Elderly's Perception of Helping Sources				
14. Turn to self	--	-.28*	-.33**	.09
15. Turn to relatives		--	.61***	-.18
16. Turn to friends			--	.26*
17. Group of friends				--

*p<.05   **p<.01   ***p<.001

INDEX